GOD
Encounters

GOD
Encounters

Stories of His Involvement in
Life's Greatest Mysteries

JAMES STUART BELL

Guideposts.org

This Guideposts edition was published by special arrangement with Howard Books, a division of Simon & Schuster, Inc.

Published by Guideposts Books & Inspirational Media
100 Reserve Road, Suite E200
Danbury, CT 06810
Guideposts.org

Acknowledgments
Every attempt has been made to credit the sources of copyrighted material used in this book. If any such acknowledgment has been inadvertently omitted or miscredited, receipt of such information would be appreciated.

All scriptures are taken from the *Holy Bible, New Living Translation,* copyright © 1996, 2004 by Tyndale Charitable Trust. Used by permission of Tyndale House Publishers, Inc., Wheaton, Illinois 60189. All rights reserved.

Library of Congress Cataloging-in-Publication Data
God encounters : stories of His involvement in life's greatest moments / compiled by James Stuart Bell.
    p. cm.
1. Christian life—Anecdotes. 2. Spirituality. I. Bell, James S.

  BV4517.G625 2009
  242—dc22

                  2009029972

Manufactured in the United States of America

Cover design by Pamela Weldon, Weldon Design LLC, wdesignstudiollc.com
Cover image from Dreamstime
Interior design by Tennille Paden
10 9 8 7 6 5 4 ⊠ 2 1

To David and Karen Mains,

who first explained

God encounters in everyday life.

CONTENTS

Contents

INTRODUCTION

*W*here is God when you need Him? You might be surprised. Because whether you see Him or not, He's right there with you—guarding, guiding, and giving you just what you need at just the right time. There is nothing on this earth like the direct experience of His loving care, His forgiveness, His comfort, His encouragement. Perhaps you hunger for His presence in life's tough circumstances and need reassurance of His unending love, personally, just for you. If you'd like a peek at God in action, then go ahead, open the pages of this book. On every page you'll find new visions of who God is and who He has created you to be.

You'll read about people who encountered God in the good times, and in the bad. In some of life's greatest moments, and in ordinary circumstances.

You'll see glimpses of God through . . .

- Sudha, who was pulled back from diving, in the dark, into an empty pool
- Jim, who learned that God is revealed even through our failings
- Pat, who saw God while bombs burst overhead
- Jon, who found evidences of the Lord in the sweet spot of a tornado
- Karen, who found God's "fingerprints" in her burgled house

- Lynn, who encountered God on her way to end her life
- Mimi, who learned from God while riding out Hurricane Katrina
- C. M., who saw the Lord in the faith of a boy with Down syndrome
- Jill, who had a visit from God in the grocery store
- David, who saw God in a newborn's smile
- Donald, who watched as his dying friend experienced God's presence

And about three dozen other people who can pinpoint faith-sustaining moments when God clearly "showed up" and brought about important changes in their lives.

What does it feel like when God breaks in and interrupts the logical flow of cause and effect or moves in quietly to answer your prayers? A sense of His abiding presence was experienced by two disciples walking with Him on the road to Emmaus. They said their hearts were strangely warmed as they recognized this true God sighting (see Luke 24:32).

Though you may not see Him with your own eyes, you, too, can experience his peace, joy, and comfort in your heart as you observe His work in His followers—people just like you whose dreams are fulfilled, relationships restored, safety protected, and debts paid off.

Perhaps you need a miracle right now or just a reminder that God cares. Perhaps you just need a nudge to look for God in your daily life or a prompting to praise Him. These stories will not only bring you into His presence but will give you fresh insight and stories to share with others who are hungering to see God at work. You can also use this book personally for fun, challenge, and renewal. Bring it into your quiet time with God, and ask Him to move in similar ways, realizing that He has a unique plan to show Himself just as powerfully to you. Or use it as a weekly reminder to look for God in your life in the days ahead. Remember the promise from His Word—*If you look for me wholeheartedly, you will find me* (Jeremiah 29:13). Find Him in these pages and in your life . . . today . . . now!

God Is Faithful

Can You Hear Me Now?

Jill Thompson

I hesitantly approached the entrance of the store. The automatic double doors slid open in a brisk and definite welcome that didn't exactly match my mood. My decision to come had been tentative at best.

I decided that if I saw anybody I knew, I'd respond to his or her greeting with a cheerful "Fine, and you?" and hope that my public demeanor would not betray the private worry I carried in my pocket. I sidestepped an abandoned shopping cart, shook off my apprehension, and entered the building bustling with people, produce, and possibility. I silently prayed I would be able to feed my husband and our five boys for the week with the ten dollars in my pocket.

The recent birth of our triplet boys had put a strain on our one-income, one-vehicle family. Still, we managed to get by for a while; that is, until the year of losses: first, my husband's health; then his job; and finally, his mental state. The latter tailspinned to a depth I could not fully understand.

In our small town, where nobody uses turn signals because everybody knows where you're going, it would have been easy to wear my woe for all to see. But I was too shy. And our predicament felt a little too personal to become the subject of pity-induced gossip that would have spread from beneath hair dryers and under car hoods.

Instead, I had quietly chosen to stand in line at social services to apply for food stamps—which were denied.

"If you sold your van," the nonchalant caseworker said with a sigh, "you'd be over the income limit. So you have too many assets to receive government assistance."

My isolation felt immense. Yet how could I feel alone when there were lots of other young mothers with mouths to feed, absent spouses, and financial burdens beyond their control?

Some people have faced even worse, much worse. I tried to talk a little truth to myself. I mean, who was I to pester God about food and health and finances when we had clean water, a roof over our heads, and lived in a free country? I wasn't so bad off.

> Who was I to pester God about food and health and finances when we had clean water, a roof over our heads, and lived in a free country?

Certainly I'd given my heart to God with no expectation of a trouble-free life in return. I began to see our family's circumstances in the light of a grand experiment, a God-given opportunity even. Could I actually live as joyfully and contented in our days of want as I had in times of plenty?

Yes, I decided. No fair-weather faith for me, even if God seemed to be acting like he hadn't heard me.

Three steps into the store, I ran into people I knew. Harold and Ruth, an elderly couple from church, had just finished shopping and were heading toward the checkout line. Though I knew these two were not overendowed with material goods, they enjoyed a wealth far beyond what money could provide. They had raised three kids, had seen hard times come and go, and still were able to live faith-filled lives.

My smile was genuine, and even my "Fine, and you?" had rung true as we visited and then continued our separate ways.

A big bag of potatoes, some oranges on sale, and milk. Now the meat department came into view. A friend of mine had told me that while she put her husband through med school, she'd served him and their two little boys cow tongue. I looked over the cellophane packages. She was right; it was cheap.

I took a long hard look and shuddered. I just couldn't do it. I moved to the generic-food aisle, hoping to select from among the black-and-white packages there.

"Jill . . . oh, there you are." It was Harold coming slowly toward me.

"Hi, Harold. I thought you and Ruth were through."

"Yep we are. She's waiting for me, but I had to ask you a question."

"Okay, what is it?"

"Do you believe that God speaks to us?"

Harold was a deacon in the church. He knew his Bible inside and out. Yet he was one of those saints who lived his faith in the real world. Was Harold testing me?

"Is this a trick question? What do you mean, like, does God talk to us while we're praying or something?" I responded.

Harold's eyes twinkled, a smile played on his lips.

"No, I mean literally, so we can hear. Do you believe that God talks to us . . . that He speaks so we can hear Him?"

I thought about that. I weighed both the positive and the negative responses I might give. A coupon-laden mother and her curly-haired, wide-eyed little girl pushed by us heading toward the meat counter. I took a chance.

"You know, Harold, I think I *do* believe that God can really speak to us. So, yes, I guess my answer is yes."

"Good. I'm glad you said that, because then you'll believe me when

God Is Faithful

I say that God just spoke to me as I was leaving the store, and He told me to give you the money in my wallet." And with that, Harold reached into his pocket and drew out his wallet. I was astonished.

Now, there have been many times in my life when another person's words or actions touched my heart in a way that made me feel unworthy to receive them. I felt like that now. I watched this precious elderly gentleman with shaky hands and arthritic knuckles fumble through his ancient wallet to extract the bills. Gently, he held them out to me.

"Harold, I . . . I . . ."

"I really heard God speak to me," he said, putting the money in my hand.

"Harold, I . . . I don't know what to say. I . . . I think I'm going to cry!"

"Buy some tissues. They're in the next aisle," he chuckled, patting my shoulder.

"Oh my . . ." The tears trickled over. I looked down at the answer to prayer in my hand. "Thank you, Harold. Just . . . thank you!" I said as he turned to go.

"See you Sunday!" He waved and continued down the aisle, disappearing around the soup display. Standing there, holding evidence of God's faithfulness, with unaware shoppers swirling around me, I felt, well . . . loved.

"I hear you, Lord." I whispered. "I know now that you value me more than the birds of the air. I hear you reminding me that if you can feed them, you will take care of us who are worth infinitely more.

"I hear you in Harold's actions. I'm reminded that nothing, not a husband's illness, not unemployment, not more kids than resources, *nothing*, separates us from your love. Not a thing!"

With contentment and even joy, I wiped my eyes with my sleeve, turned my shopping cart around, and joined the wide-eyed girl and her mother at the meat counter.

God Is Protector

ANGEL IN FLIGHT

Veronica Rose

I must not oversleep, I thought as I set the alarm for 4:00 a.m. and crawled into bed.

I lay in the darkness considering the events of the past year. Since the demon of alcohol had invaded our home, everything had changed. I felt at times I was just trying to hang on to my own sanity, as I saw my husband, Andy, becoming more and more delusional and irrational. He certainly was not the Andy I had married twenty years earlier. Under the influence of alcohol, he had changed from an optimistic, fun-loving guy to a person I didn't recognize.

I had to take on the responsibility for the welfare of our family, despite frequently feeling helpless and untrained for this journey. Alcohol had never been in my home or on the scene with my friends, so for many weeks I didn't know how to spot the obvious fact that Andy had started drinking.

Beside me, Andy lay snoring softly, oblivious to my worries and concerns. Sleep seemed as foreign to my brain as the pathway I had traveled this past year, trying to learn how to respond to the quirks and paranoia of an alcoholic.

Andy was scheduled to enter an alcoholic treatment center in Boston for thirty days. In the morning our nephew would take him to the airport. He was lined up to change planes in New York, but I was apprehensive. I suspected he would take advantage of the opportunity to have a few last drinks, and I worried he would not be sober enough to get on the correct flight. Where would he end up? Would he follow through on this plan, or would he call for someone to come and get him and take him elsewhere?

I needed to find a release for all these fears; so quietly, hoping not to disturb him, I eased out of bed and tiptoed to the living room. My faithful old rocking chair seemed to be waiting for me that night, as it had many nights lately. Just rocking gently back and forth always brought me calmness as I let go of my anxieties, at least for the moment.

I had been a Christian for twenty years, but this past year my faith had been tested in a way I would never have imagined. Through it all, the Lord had been my strength and comfort, and I believed He had much better things for Andy and me and our family. I could not, nor

> With tears, I asked God to send
> an angel to ride with Andy to watch over him.

would I ever, settle for the disorder and upheaval that threatened our family's happiness.

I sat in my rocking chair in the still night and asked God to take all my fears and frustrations and bring us back to a family living in harmony again. With tears, I asked God to send an angel to ride with Andy and watch over him.

"Please get him safely to his destination and bring him back a new man," I begged.

I looked at the clock as I crawled back under the covers. It was 1:30 in the morning. I felt at peace. Now I knew I could sleep.

Andy returned from the treatment center as a new, happy, and healthy man, and a year later he still had no desire to tempt the alcoholic demons. He talked frequently about the programs he went through, and at one point he said, "They couldn't believe that I arrived with no alcohol in my system. Most people arrive really pickled, because they know it's the last time they get to drink."

"How did you arrive free of alcohol? Didn't you drink on the plane?" I finally asked.

He hadn't spoken about the flight, except when he called from the airport that morning to tell me his flight was canceled. He had asked me to call the treatment center and tell them he would come on another flight. The other flight would not include changing planes in New York. I was so relieved and grateful. I knew one prayer had been answered.

Now he picked up the story as he said, "I need to tell you about that flight. It was very strange and a bit aggravating. I got on the plane, fully intending to have some last drinks before I arrived. But before I could order a drink, this congenial lady came down the aisle and sat beside me. She told me some things about herself and said she was going to a church conference in Boston.

"She asked me what my mission was in Boston, but I hedged a bit. As she continued to talk to me and tell me about the great God we serve, I just couldn't bring myself to drink in front of her. So I only had an orange juice. It was really strange. You would've thought she was assigned to me, or something. She never left my side the entire flight."

By this time I was nearly jumping up and down with joy.

"But she *was* assigned to you," I exclaimed. "She was an answer to my prayers! Why didn't you tell me this sooner?"

Andy looked at me, somewhat perplexed. "How did you know that woman?"

God Is Protector

"I didn't, but God did. He heard my prayer that morning before you left," I said. "He looked out for you just as I asked Him to!"

"Well, she certainly did get under my skin. I was in no mood to talk, but I had to respond to her or appear rude." He removed his glasses and started to clean them with his handkerchief as he continued. "Her demeanor was so nonthreatening and genuine that even though I didn't want to talk, I found her conversation calming and encouraging."

I watched as he placed his glasses back on, and I said, "Isn't it wonderful to see God in action like that? She was like an angel from God. An answer to my prayers."

"Yes," he nodded, "and now it all makes sense to me. I just couldn't understand why she seemed so concerned about my welfare.

"She did her assignment well," he added with a chuckle.

"God knows how to handle tough situations, even if we might have our doubts," I said, as I squeezed Andy's arm.

MIRACLE IN MOTION

Renae Brumbaugh

*M*iscarriage is a fact of life. It happens to a lot of people, right? It is sad and disappointing, but you deal with it. You move on. Or at least that's what I thought before it happened to me.

I didn't realize that with the premature death of my baby, I would also mourn the loss of something intangible, unspoken. When my baby died, hope died. At that point, I entered a black tunnel of grief and despair that was beyond description.

Somehow, I kept moving. But I can't really say I kept living in the fullest sense. My life took on a robotlike quality. I moved, I spoke, I did what was required; but there was no spark, no depth.

I attended church and tried to be the perfect android pastor's wife, smiling and nodding, trying to remember names, trying to say and do all the right things. But the protective shell I had placed around my heart was a thin one and was in danger of cracking at any moment.

I didn't eat or sleep. All I really did was cry. Not the deep, heart-wrenching sobs that stem from great emotion. Instead, silent tears slid down my face so often that I almost stopped noticing them. Most days, I stayed in my pajamas. Some Sundays, I didn't even have the strength to get dressed and go to church. I just couldn't do it.

I quit talking to God. I was mad at Him. I couldn't understand why He had played such a dirty trick on me: first, with years of infertility, then dangling my baby in front of me only to take him away. And I didn't want to hear from God, either. I was so angry with Him; I didn't really care what He had to say.

Late one night, I woke Mark from a deep sleep. "Sweetheart, I have to tell you something." He sat up groggily and squinted at me.

"I know this will be hard for you, because you're a pastor. But I've decided not to have a relationship with God anymore."

He blinked at me. Long silence. Finally, he asked, "Just like that? You're going to stop loving God?"

I looked at him like he was nuts. "Stop loving Him? I never said that! God knows I love Him with all my heart! I just don't think He loves *me*. And I can't handle that, so I'm going to cut all ties with Him."

> The protective shell I had placed around my heart was a thin one and was in danger of cracking at any moment.

Long, thick silence. Finally, he spoke. "Well . . . don't be *too* mean to Him. He is my boss, you know." And he rolled over and went back to sleep.

So began my life without God. Or at least my attempt. Have you ever tried to ignore someone, but they just wouldn't leave you alone? That's what God did to me. He kept whispering words of love and comfort into my spirit, and I kept pushing Him away. I didn't want to hear them.

Eventually, I got sick. It started out as a cold, but I couldn't shake it, so I went to see a doctor. A soft-spoken woman, she gently questioned me about my health. Before I knew it, I was sobbing and pouring out my whole sad story to her. She listened and handed me tissues. Finally she spoke, and her words shocked me to my core.

"You have postpartum depression." *Postpartum depression? I thought that only happened to women who gave birth! I never dreamed it could happen after a miscarriage!*

She continued. "I'm going to write you a prescription for an antidepressant."

I snapped to attention. "No! I really don't want to take an antidepressant. I . . . I guess deep down I'm still hoping I'll get pregnant again. I don't want to take anything that could harm my baby."

She eyed me for several long moments. "Then I'm going to insist that you seek professional counseling. Your insurance will pay for it. But you can't keep going on this way, not eating, not sleeping. You probably shouldn't even be driving."

I was that bad, huh? I didn't think it was that obvious. I looked at the doctor, then down at my feet. "Okay, I'll go to a counselor."

I thumbed through the phone book and found the name of a counselor in DeRidder, just one town over. Close enough to drive and far enough to avoid prying eyes and wagging tongues. A few days later I drove myself to the counseling office.

I was given a questionnaire to fill out. It asked all the standard health questions. Then it got personal: *Are you suicidal?*

That question nearly leaped off the page at me. *Was I?* Perhaps. I certainly felt dead already. I wanted to die, for that would be better than the deep pain and depression. That would be better than the rejection I felt from God.

Hesitantly, I circled *yes.*

I finished the questionnaire. I was about to turn it in when I remembered something I'd learned years before, in a college counseling class. Something about suicidal patients. What was it again? Was the counselor required by law to notify the authorities or family members or something? Oh, great. Just what I needed. Our whole town lining the streets to watch the strait-jacketed preacher's wife being driven

God Is Comforter

off to the looney farm. I found the suicide question and changed my answer to *no*.

The counselor was an attractive woman in her forties. She wore a tan pantsuit. I remember wishing my legs were as long as hers. Good grief! I was in the middle of a life crisis! I guess vanity dies hard.

I was uncomfortable at first as she began to ask a few questions. But before long, she had me feeling at ease.

"You've been through a lot," she said. "Infertility alone can be devastating. So can a miscarriage."

"But I feel like I should be handling it all better," I told her.

"Don't be so hard on yourself," she responded. "Give yourself some time. I am concerned that you're not sleeping, though. You can't continue this way. I want you to start exercising."

Exercising? Was the woman nuts? I didn't care about losing the baby weight or anything else. The last thing I wanted was to attend some peppy aerobics class with some cute little instructor named Kimmi telling me to "Make it burn!"

She could see I was hesitant, but she kept insisting. Finally, I agreed to try walking a few minutes each day. I was glad the insurance was paying for this. Fifty dollars an hour to be told to walk. Sheesh! I was expecting something a little more life changing.

But walk, I did. And I had a walking buddy—God. During those walks, I could hear Him talking to me. And without all my usual distractions, I was forced to listen.

He told me He loved me, He knew I was hurting, and that He was hurting too. He whispered to me and wooed me and before long I surrendered. With tears streaming down my face, I finally told God, "Look. I don't know what You're doing. I don't have any idea why You took my baby or what You have in store. None of it seems right or fair to me. But, okay God. I give up. I surrender. I'm going to trust You."

With those words, a release button was pressed somewhere deep in my soul. All the grief finally had a place to go. Slowly but surely, the heartache that had been festering within me began to disappear.

Oh, it wasn't instant. But healing had begun. I still cried myself to sleep at night. But sleep came.

One night, as I turned my tear-soaked pillow to the dry side, I heard a voice. Not an audible voice, but a clear one nonetheless. Somewhere in the recesses of my mind I heard the voice of God whisper, *If you only knew what I have in store for you just around the corner, you wouldn't be crying.*

Surely, I was losing my mind.

Just two days later, I ran into Josh at church. Josh was a young army recruit stationed at Fort Polk, near Leesville. He had also been

> If you only knew what I have in store for you just around the corner, you wouldn't be crying.

a member of our former church in Copperas Cove, Texas. His family still lived there.

We made small talk. I asked about his family and specifically about his sixteen-year-old cousin, Lilly.

"Funny you should mention her," Josh said. "I spoke to Mom and Dad yesterday, and they told me she's pregnant."

"Oh, I see . . ." I replied. "What does she plan to do?"

"She's considering adoption. Oh, look at the time. We'd better go or we'll be late for the service."

I stood there, watching him walk away, my heart pounding, struggling to breathe. I somehow found my way into the sanctuary and sat in my usual pew. But my mind was not on the service or on my husband's sermon. Josh's words kept spinning in my head. *She wants to give the baby up for adoption. She wants to give the baby up for adoption.*

God Is Comforter

I couldn't hope. Could I? No, surely not. It could never work. Could it? *Please God. Please don't let me hope. Please don't let me think there is a chance if there isn't.*

Could it work, God? I want this child, God. Please give us this child. Please, God.

At the close of the service, I nearly ran over several dear church members, trying to find Josh. I caught up with him in the parking lot. I had no idea what to say to the young man. He'd probably think I was nuts. And he would be right. But I had nothing to lose.

"Josh!" He turned in my direction. "I wanted to talk to you about Lilly. I, um, well . . . you may know that Mark and I recently lost a baby."

His eyes were compassionate. "Yes, ma'am. I'm very sorry about that."

"We're thinking of adopting. Would you mind just mentioning that to your parents?"

He smiled. "I'll call them this afternoon."

"Thanks," I whispered.

What have I done? I haven't even talked to Mark. What have I done, Lord?

That afternoon, I told Mark about the conversation. He responded with, "We'll see what happens." Calm and detached. A typical man.

At 3:04 p.m., the phone rang. It was Paul and Nancy McGee, Josh's parents. I wish I could give you a word-for-word account of the conversation, but I can't. All I really remember is that somehow, the ball started rolling. That conversation set into motion a miracle, a child that satisfied the deepest desires of my heart.

God Is Teacher

DIARY OF A GUITAR . . . JOURNEY OF A PRAYER

Sandi Banks

*L*et's see, suitcase . . . check . . . missionaries' peanut butter, tuna, donated clothes . . . check. Bibles, books, guitar, song sheets . . . check . . .

The packing frenzy had begun for my sixteen-year-old daughter and me. Soon we would wing our way to Rwanda, Africa, on our church's summer mission trip. Our team of twenty-two teens and five leaders had spent the past year planning and training for this adventure. *Denver to New York to Paris to Africa and back.* I tried to mentally process it all.

Praying about all the unknowns and crosscultural encounters ahead, I grew increasingly excited at the thought of meaningful ministry. And I had the distinct sense that God was prompting me to take one item to leave in Africa: my beloved guitar.

This was no ordinary instrument, in my mind. It was special. Not just because of its large size, full sound, or polished mahogany inlays, but because, more important, it had been my co-laborer in ministry. For more than twenty-five years, my "friend" had been Velcroed to my body, as it were. It had served me well over the years, strumming folk songs and silly show tunes on bumpy buses and jostling jeep rides, assisting my six- and seven-year-olds' Joyful Noise choir, and tromping with me through more than two decades of music ministry experiences around the globe.

I ran my hand slowly across the sounding board, remembering a balmy evening years earlier on a Mexican beach. We'd had an impromptu praisefest, when the Christian college choral group heard our group singing "love songs to Jesus" from across the water and joined us on the moonlit sand, enriching our worship with their glorious harmonies. I could almost hear and smell and touch and taste that evening all over again—the soft guitar strums and rhythmic laps of ocean waves creating the perfect backdrop for our adoration of our awesome God. And this guitar friend had been right there with me.

Ah, the memories! And so many more for which I was thankful. But now I needed to tuck them away again and return to the business at hand. Packing the guitar with care, I prayed God would show me what to do with it when we got to Africa.

But first He had a few final assignments for the two of us.

> Packing the guitar with care,
> I prayed God would show me what to do
> with it when we got to Africa.

Our team of twenty-seven arrived in this picturesque "Switzerland of Africa" in the heat of midday and hit the ground running. We had much to do. We had a church to tear down and a church to build. We had people to meet, schools to visit, children to minister to, huge open-air evangelistic meetings, and small-village Sunday services. We were to participate in festive national parades as well as simple reflective times on the shores of Lake Kivu. We had gospel messages and testimonies to share, relationships to form with our new Rwandan friends and so much more.

And in the midst of it all was *music*.

Music laced the long days of bricklaying and tree hauling—with curious onlookers dotting the hillside surrounding our work site.

The long days were followed by nightly services under the banana trees: testimonies, sermons, and you guessed it, praise songs with the guitar.

Music filled the miles as we traveled by open trucks from village to village. We sang and strummed along the way, while the waving folks beside the road eagerly received our evangelistic booklets.

Music laced the long Sunday-morning services, which were wonderfully warmed and softened by lovable saints and jubilant singing.

Everywhere we went, I wondered: *Could this be the place?*

Like the starry night, I stood with my guitar atop a high platform overlooking the crowd with our translator, Saba, by my side. Thousands had gathered below for the first of two nights to see the *Jesus* film, to hear the gospel message over loudspeakers—and to sing.

The gentle African breezes nuzzled my face and ruffled the hem of my long skirt. I felt strangely warm, and at peace. Gazing up into the vast dark sky glittered with its millions of white stars, and below, at the sea of beautiful faces with the thousands of bright eyes, I couldn't help but marvel at God's majestic splendor and goodness.

Then it was time. Lifting the guitar, I stepped up to the microphone on the tiny platform, smiled, and called out, "Turarimba twese!" (*"Let us sing together!"*) Suddenly the crowd erupted into loud shouting and stomping, thrusting their fists into the air. I was terrified! Turning to Saba, I shouted above the din,

"What's happening? What did I say wrong?"

He grinned. "No, ees good! They never hear Muzoongoo speak their language."

And so we did indeed "sing together."

Ye nahee semu, Kubua Jesu . . . Nha bgonza su birinyuma.

I have decided to follow Jesus . . . no turning back.

Inshutzi zanja, zosay zanyanga . . . Nha bgonza su birinyuma.

God Is Teacher

Though none go with me, still I will follow . . . no turning back.

Verse after verse, song after song, my guitar faithfully fulfilled its role.

Thousands of voices, lifted in praise and worship, filled the open air and the depths of my soul. Surely this was a glimpse of a heavenly host choir rehearsal!

But something in my spirit told me that this was not yet the place.

The following Sunday at the large Nyaga-henica church where my daughter gave her poignant testimony, I wondered, *Is this the place, Lord?*

I wondered as we neared our last week, putting final touches on the rafters and roof of our building project, and as we interacted with people. I prayed, *Where, Lord, where?*

On our final Sunday we split into three groups. The group I was in trekked to a small town called Nyaga-gesenja, an hour away. The congregation was friendly and particularly eager to sing, as I stood up front and strummed the familiar songs.

Then it happened—the unmistakable prompting: *Here. This is the place!*

I lifted the strap and tenderly held the guitar in front of me. Smiling, looking into the eyes of these precious saints, and with Saba interpreting, I said, "This guitar has played hymns and love songs to Jesus for many years. Now, on behalf of all of us from America, I would like to present this guitar to you as a gift, so that you, too, can . . . "

As soon as Saba translated the word "gift," the people burst into tears of joy and shouts of "Hallelujah!" They hugged one another and raised their hands in praise. This time I knew it was a "good" outburst—I just had no idea for the reason behind it.

I was soon to learn: these folks had *prayed for seven years for a guitar.*

What an indescribable honor, to be part of God's answer to a seven-year prayer, from halfway around the world! I thought back to the packing, His clear tugging on my heart to give away my guitar, the daily wondering, waiting! I stood rejoicing with these dear, oh-so-persistent-in-prayer people and joined them in their tears of joy.

No one knew how to play a guitar! They just knew it was the desire of their hearts. With a few whirlwind lessons, we soon found that the director, Yohance, would master the instrument and minister in music.

> What an indescribable honor, to be part of
> God's answer to a seven-year prayer,
> from halfway around the world!

I'm sitting here looking at a favorite photo of Yohance with his big guitar and his even bigger grin. It was the last time I ever saw my old friend, my guitar. But it looks mighty at home in the arms of its new owner.

To *God* be all the glory—He who is faithful to hear a prayer in one corner of the world and tug at a heart in another.

Dare we ever wonder if He is able?

God Is Teacher

God Is Refuge

THE SWEET SPOT

Jon Hopkins

*I*t was a dark and stormy night. No, really, it was—except it was only three o'clock on a spring afternoon in 2006.

"I can't see," I said, holding the video camera.

Sean, my brother-in-law and owner of Blown Away Storm Excursion Tours, grasped the steering wheel as we drove into the storm's center. "Just keep filming. Keep filming."

"How can you see?" I asked.

"Just have to look for the telephone poles. As long as they are on the right, I know I'm still on the road."

I trusted Sean. We had chased many storms together. I was in my regular place videoing from the passenger's seat. In front of me was a laptop showing current radar and our position in the storm.

"Warning," the computer flashed, "you are approaching a dangerous storm."

"What's happening now?" Sean said in his usual calm voice.

That was my job—to tell him where we were and what was happening on the radar. I was the "nowcaster."

I looked at the computer to check the radar/GPS. "We can turn south in one mile," I said.

Lightning flashed.

"Wow, look at that!" Sean pointed out the window.

As I looked out the window of our new Chevy Trailblazer at the many hail dents on the hood, I noticed the antenna was bent all the way down over the hood by the wind, at a ninety-degree angle from the direction we were heading.

"How fast are you going?"

"Eighty or so."

I sucked in air between my teeth. That meant the crosswind was stronger than the speed we were going. It was a wonder he could keep us on the road. I looked at the radar. Somewhere in the dark, to the left of us, was a tornado. As the hail started to hit the car, we turned south.

"Hey, just lay off the gas and let the wind take us down the road," I said, when I saw the horizontal rain outside my window. We both laughed. We were in the core of the storm where the rain is the heaviest and the hail is large and loud. But in less than two minutes we had punched through the core and had emerged into bright sunlight. Sean pulled off the road somewhere near Yuma, Colorado. We calmly stood alongside the road and watched the tornadic storm.

"Man, Sean, you're the best. You always get us to the sweet spot." The sweet spot is that place where you can watch nature's fury in safety.

The next season was much different.

On April 21, 2007, we were traveling west, furiously trying to catch up to a line of storms heading into Dumas, Texas. The radar showed multiple rotations. This storm was dropping tornados right and left. It was going to be an exciting chase. Sean put in his favorite Kenny Loggins CD, and it blared "Highway to the Danger Zone."

"There it is!" I cried, pointing to the south. I could see the tornado tearing up the ground in the distance. Shaped like a large bowl—wedge shaped—it was trailing alongside us at about the same speed we were traveling.

"Wooohoo! Look at that!" I felt the excitement in the backseat as

God Is Refuge

our passengers scrambled for their cameras. This was their first tornado. They pushed their foreheads to the window glass. It started to rain.

"It's getting bigger!" one of the passengers yelled. "It must be an F4!" They slapped hands in the air.

Sean looked at me, and I could see by the fear in his eyes that he was thinking the same thing I was. Tornados don't usually grow bigger. It was an optical illusion that occurs when the track changes and the tornado heads straight toward you. It was bearing right down on us and would meet us on the road ahead.

> ### It was bearing right down on us and would meet us on the road ahead.

"I think we should stop right here," I said, trying to sound calm, "and let it just go by us."

"Y'know, it is kinda coming right at us," Sean said, "and it's getting rain wrapped."

That meant the tornado was embedded in the storm and you couldn't see it for the rain. I grabbed the video camera tighter and clenched my teeth.

Okay, I thought, *it's time to find the sweet spot.*

"I want to go south," Sean said as we reached a gravel road. Turning the wheel sharply, he tried to get behind the tornado. About two hundred yards down the road he said, "This is mud! I can't even stop."

The road was wet clay. It was slicker than ice. The wheels turned. I could see the tornado shifting to the right. It had grown powerful. I have always heard people say that tornados sound like trains, but all I could hear was the sound of trees cracking and the howling wind. And all I could smell was mud.

"Need to turn around," Sean said, as he put the car in reverse. The tornado acted like it anticipated the move and turned so that we were in the outflow wind path. Sean gunned the car, and every time he did, the wind and the slick road shifted us ever closer to a huge ravine on the side of the road. One more try, and the SUV almost tipped over as we slid quickly down into the ravine.

Sean put the vehicle into four-wheel drive and tried to move forward. The engine roared. Wheels spun. Mud splashed up over the windshield and blocked our view. The car didn't budge. We couldn't move. I could hear cameras clicking and heavy breathing from the backseat. I watched Sean, thinking, *C'mon, you gotta get us outta here!*

Leaning into the steering wheel, head forward, eyes squinted tight enough that I could see lines on his temples—he was fighting the mud for his life. Our lives. My life.

He turned on the wipers again just in time to see another tornado drop in front of us and a little to the left. Two tornados were now on the ground. The new tornado was thin, silver white, ropelike, and beautiful against the gunmetal sky and bright green field. The passengers forgot about the rain-wrapped tornado coming directly at us and began photographing the "pretty little tornado" as it passed into the field.

I passed my camera back to someone and turned to look through the mud, hoping the big one had disappeared. I held my breath as I rolled down the window. The big tornado was about two blocks away.

Trying to rock the car back out of the ditch, all Sean noticed was the rushing water rising in the ravine and the flash flood heading our way. As the torrent hit the car, I felt water splash in through the window. I turned the video camera off and set it aside.

My heart pounded. The sounds of the wind and rushing water pushed aside all rational thoughts in my head. I felt the drop of

God Is Refuge

pressure from the approaching tornado on the hairs of my arm. I don't remember ever being as afraid as I was just then. Punching the core of a storm the year before seemed peaceful compared to this.

I tried to talk. My throat was dry. The car began to rock side to side. The inflow winds pushed us, like a mother rocking a cradle. Back and forth we went. Forward and back, but the rocking brought no comfort.

I thought I was going to die. I put my hands over my face and heard myself cry out, "God, save us!"

At that moment, Sean shifted the car into reverse, and we lurched backward. The tires had grabbed hold of something. And then I saw the wedge tornado lift to the clouds above just as it hit the clay-covered road next to us. Mud flew high into the air. I heard the clods hit the roof of the vehicle as we inched backward toward the paved road.

When we finally got to the road, the wind and rain had completely stopped. I opened the door and saw a teenage boy standing by his bright blue pickup truck on the crossroad. Had he been there the whole time? I heard him say, "Wow . . . Wow . . . Wow." and "Ha! I got it all on tape!"

Everyone else got out of the vehicle to look around. They were laughing and shaking their arms, perhaps to shake off the goose bumps. Our passengers shared the adrenaline rush as they ran down the street to see where the small rope tornado had crossed the road.

Me? I looked down the clay road where we had been stuck in the mud. Someone had once said, "A rut is a grave with both ends kicked out." That could've been my grave right there.

Was it circumstance? I thought. No, circumstance got us into the situation, but it didn't get us out of it. All I could think of was my prayer and the exact moment the tornado disappeared and the exact moment the car moved. I realized right then that no matter where I was, whatever danger I would face, I would always know where the sweet spot really was. It's being in the shadow of His wings, when His everlasting arms are underneath us.

I looked to Sean, who was sadly looking at his Trailblazer. I wondered if he realized what God had just done for us.

Obviously not. "We gotta find a carwash!" he moaned.

God Is Refuge

God Is Redeemer

BECAUSE OF A FALLEN TREE

Sally Edwards Danley

"*S*ally, sit still!" Having my hair jerked, as Mom braided it, hurt so much it made my eyes fill with tears. But I held them back. I'd begged to not have braids, but Mom hadn't acquiesced. In fact, she acted like she enjoyed yanking my hair.

As a quiet little kid, I never got spankings. But I got enough scolding and criticism from Mom to feel punished. "Stand up straight!" "Don't chew your nails!" "Can't you do anything right?" "No, I won't teach you how to make cocoa. You'll just mess up the kitchen."

She never complimented me. No wonder I lacked self-confidence. I was a timid little girl who stood off by myself, chewing my fingernails.

My parents were taught it was harmful to touch your child too much. So we never enjoyed hugging and physical nurturing. In fact, I never even heard "I love you" from my parents until I was past thirty years old.

Balancing out Mom's criticisms, Daddy was an honest, gentle man who always treated me with respect and listened to me. We carried on meaningful conversations.

As I reached my late teens, I fell in love with an affectionate young man who became my husband. His affectionate touching made such a difference in my life—his demonstrative care made me feel positive about myself for the first time in my life. And later I made sure my three children were hugged and told they were loved.

After our little family moved several hundred miles away from my parents, I began to greet Mom and Daddy with a hug whenever we went home to visit them.

My marriage ended when my three children were teens. While I'd grown to hate my mother more and more as an adult, I often called my daddy for advice. Five years later, when he died, I was a new grandmother and sole supporter of my teens and the baby. I missed my daddy terribly. Over the next few years I fussed at God, "Why did you have to take Daddy? Why didn't you take Mom?"

As the children continued to grow and my nest emptied, that old self-doubt I'd endured as a child returned, and I began working with a psychotherapist. He suggested I look into an Adult Children of Alcoholics group.

"But my parents hardly drank more than a glass of wine a year," I responded. He pointed out that perhaps my parents had been raised by alcoholics; my mother's cruel behavior compared to that of an abused child of an alcoholic. Mom had spoken little about her parents.

At these Adult Children of Alcoholics meetings, I met others who had suffered similar childhood abuse. My attitude changed. I saw how Mom's twisted concepts had distorted truth for me. It felt as if my eyes had been opened to the light after living in darkness all my life. I understood myself as never before.

Years passed, and I realized one day that I no longer felt anger and resentment toward Mom. My trips to visit her became more pleasant.

After Daddy's death, my brothers had tried to get Mom to move out of the old homestead and into a retirement center. She stubbornly refused. They had to maintain Mom's house, as well as their own homes, for twenty-five years. At that time my mother was handling her own finances, although she knew nothing about budgeting.

God Is Redeemer

Then came the unexpected. During a major windstorm, a tree fell on her old house, destroying half of the roof and the back entryway. The house insurance had expired because Mom had not paid the premiums. My brothers would have to repair the building in their spare time. They both had jobs and their own families, so that meant it would take a long time.

One brother moved Mom in with his family for a time. But when a rental house he owned was vacant, he quickly moved her there. His nineteen-year-old son decided to live with Mom, but she did not welcome his friends who came and went frequently, staying late into the night. Nor did she approve of his blaring music. She was used to a quiet home and solitude.

A month after the tree fell, I visited Mom and the old house. The extent of the damage overwhelmed me. It was worse than I'd imagined. I remembered our beautiful backyard where Mom and Daddy had grown vegetables and fragrant flowers and where we'd had family gatherings. Our lovely, huge shade tree was now a giant stump with chunks of the cut-up trunk scattered over the gardens. Plastic covered where the door and roof had been. I left in tears.

> "I'm going home with you until they fix my roof."

When I saw Mom at the rental house, she was unusually quiet and seemed very stressed. I understood. She'd lived in the old house more than forty years. She preferred the familiar surroundings. The next day when I was leaving, instead of hugging me good-bye, she stepped into another room and returned with her purse and a suitcase.

"What are you doing?" I asked.

"I'm going home with you until they fix my roof. I can't keep living with a teenager and all that noise."

I knew better than to argue with her. Once she made a decision, she was as stubborn as a mule. I had sent her letters telling her about my pleasant neighborhood and new two-bedroom apartment where I lived alone.

It was as if God had said, *Okay, Sally, you've done all the mental work to forgive your mother, now let's put it into practice.*

After a week, I realized we had to make some changes. I turned the spare room I used as an office into Mom's bedroom. I moved my computer beside my dresser, which made my bedroom seem tight. For the first time in our lives, my eighty-three-year-old mom and I began developing a comfortable life together. We had our head-banging sessions, but surprisingly, life became fairly pleasant. We easily slipped into a bedtime hug routine.

My grown children started coming to see me more often. The two who lived in our city came to know my mom as a loving old woman. She mellowed into a more pleasant person. She no longer seemed critical. She acted pleased when my grandchildren wanted to sit in her lap, and actually hugged them. Maybe God was working on Mom while He worked on me. We had some good family times together, and her help with the basic expenses reduced some of my financial stress.

While Mom lived with me, she grew to totally depend on me and exhibited signs of agoraphobia. She refused to leave my apartment with anyone but me. My children tried to get her to go shopping or riding with them, but she wouldn't. When I had an eldercare person visit, Mom let the woman know I was all she needed for friendship or transportation.

Her total reliance on me was sometimes overwhelming.

When I had an opportunity to attend a weekend retreat without

God Is Redeemer

her, I felt trapped. Who would take care of Mom? Faithfully attending my twelve-step meetings and church helped me deal with problems as they arose. I learned to go ahead and do what I needed to do for my well-being. Surprisingly, she encouraged me to go on that and other retreats. So I did.

Over time, I came to feel love and affection for Mom. Then one evening, as we hugged goodnight, Mom stepped back and looked at me. She kissed my cheek. She had never done that before.

"Sally," she said, "I'm so glad that tree fell on my house. Otherwise I wouldn't have come to know you as an adult."

Then she said, "I love you, Sally," for the first time. What a treasured moment!

The tree might have fallen on the house because of high winds. And Mom may not have been able to have the house fixed right away because she'd failed to pay the insurance. But thanks to those problems, I saw God's blessing. He used a fallen tree to show me my mother's love.

God Is Patient

WHERE WE FAIL, GOD SUCCEEDS

Jim Rawdon

As I jumped across the creek, instead of landing on dry ground, as I'd intended, I came down in the creek's muddy edge.

A swear word popped out of my mouth. Nobody was around to hear my offensive exclamation—except for the one person who mattered. I immediately prayed, "God, forgive me."

As a sixteen-year-old high school junior, I had finally grasped what it meant to give myself wholly to God and His will. A couple of weeks earlier, I'd decided to commit my life to God.

But still, practically from day one, as on the day when I'd decided to go fishing, I struggled with the problem of swearing. In the years to come, although I often didn't say the words, I often thought them or muttered them under my breath.

After high school came college, and halfway through college came marriage. Barely a year later twin boys arrived. Supporting a family of four while maintaining a full load of college courses required my holding as many as three part-time jobs. Finding time for study, caring for babies crying with colic, and balancing work demands created frustration. I was an adult, a husband, and father. In times of pressure the desire to dismiss circumstances with profane or vulgar words often sprang to mind.

Ten years later we moved to Memphis for me to manage a men's clothing business. The move doubled my income but was hurried, so instead of buying a house, we leased a townhouse. After a year I found a foreclosed house nearby and bought it. The grass and weeds in the fenced backyard had grown to over three feet. Shortly after we took possession of the house, I stayed home from the office one Saturday. I was determined and went out to chop down that baby forest growing in the backyard to a height where I could mow it.

A new neighbor across the street saw me hacking away and came over with a six-pack of beer and said, "Hi, I'm Pat. Need a little help?" I accepted readily but declined his offer of a "cold one."

We shared our backgrounds and a little family info. Pat said, "Gloria and I grew up here in Memphis. We have two grown sons still at home." I was intrigued to learn that one was an underwater welder.

I told him "We have three. Brent and Bruce are twins in the seventh grade. The third, Page, is in the fifth. We moved up here from a little town in north Texas. My wife's going to Memphis State and trying to finish a degree in accounting."

After a couple of hours the grass and weeds were down to a level where I could mow. I thanked Pat for his unexpected and appreciated help. After he left, I began the slow job of making the broken stubble look like a yard again.

In spite of that initial involvement, Pat and I never became close friends, just friendly neighbors. We'd wave across the street and shout a hello, but I left early every day to hold morning sales meetings and usually got home late.

Shortly after the move, we joined a church nearby. Our whole family attended weekly Bible study and worship on Sundays. On Wednesdays the boys attended teens' and boys' activity groups at church, while Glenda and I went to choir practice. As our choir prepared the church's Easter musical, the director asked me to sing the tenor solos for the "Doubting Thomas" character. I replied only half-joking, "That's typecasting," but accepted the role.

In spite of regular participation in church, after I started the new job, the swearing increased. The bookkeeper insisted on an answer for why the tie inventory was off by eight hundred. *Bleep* sprang to mind. Scanning a salesman's weekly report, I realized several hundred dollars in payments was missing. My jaw clenched, and I barely stopped myself from muttering what I thought. When I realized I would have to take the report to the airport to ensure its overnight delivery, I was ashamed of what I snarled as I stomped out to my car.

More than just a temptation, swearing became a shameful pattern. On the morning of the Easter musical, I stood before the bathroom mirror, shaving. As I stroked away the shaving cream, I sensed God's Spirit pressing into my awareness. His desire for me was clear. He

Swearing became a shameful pattern.

urged me to confess my sinful weakness to my church and ask for their prayers. I needed their added strength to break this unholy habit.

When the cantata ended, our pastor asked, "Does anyone have anything he or she wants to say?"

When he glanced back toward the choir loft, I held up my hand, and he motioned for me to come forward, then handed me his microphone. I was ready to share the clear, strong impression that God wanted me to confess my moral failing to my church. So I said, "I need you folks to pray for me. All my life I've struggled against the impulse to swear. But it's become so bad that I even swear sometimes in front of my children. Please pray for me."

A few weeks after that Sunday, I was in the kitchen, pouring my morning cup of coffee. Through the kitchen window I saw Pat, the neighbor across the street, come out to drive to work. Before he reached his car, he suddenly collapsed. I was less than half dressed, so

God Is Patient

I hurried to jump into some clothes. But before I could get dressed, his two adult sons rushed out, lifted him, and led him back into the house.

I didn't know what to make of what I'd seen. I didn't want to be nosey and intrude in a family problem. We hardly knew each other except for whacking down weeds for an hour or two. Had it been a heart attack? A stroke?

I remembered the six-pack on a Saturday morning; it had seemed a little early. Could the collapse be evidence of drunkenness or alcoholism? It wasn't impossible.

For nearly two months I never saw Pat, but I did notice that his stay-at-home wife started leaving every morning. Had they separated? Had she taken a job to support herself? Then one Saturday Pat came out of their house using *a walker*. I hurried across the street and asked, "Pat, what happened?"

I'll never forget Pat's answer. "Oh, Jim, I almost bought the farm. I had a blood clot that ran all the way from my ankle to my groin and eventually got loose and went to my heart. I was in intensive care for forty-seven days. The only thing that brought me through and kept me alive was my wife's prayers."

I apologized that I hadn't known and determined to pray for him and Gloria and for his full recovery. What he had said about his wife's prayers stuck in my mind. I wondered how to respond. I decided to fix a fancy dessert of baked pears in a grenadine sauce and take it over as a gesture of caring.

That evening I carried over my dessert offering, hoping they'd be impressed, and rang their doorbell. When Pat opened the door, I explained this was my belated way of showing a little concern. They cheerfully invited me in.

I'd never been in their house before, but after a little small talk I said, "Pat, this morning you mentioned that the only thing that brought you through your heart attack was your wife's prayers. That caught my attention because prayers don't mean much unless there's a God to answer them. I mention that because I wondered if you all are active in a church. If you're not, I wanted to invite you to ours."

Pat glanced at Gloria and then said, "We'd been talking about starting to go to church before the heart attack. In fact, we had just visited a church up on Austin Peay Highway and the craziest thing happened. They had this big music program for Easter. It was impressive. The choir and all the singers were garbed in Bible-times outfits with fake beards and wigs.

"After it was over and before the benediction, the preacher asked if there were any comments. One of the singers held up his hand and came out of the choir. Then he told the church that he needed them to pray for him about cussing in front of his kids, because he couldn't stop. When I heard that, I elbowed Gloria and said, 'Sounds just like me, doesn't it?' Made me feel at home!"

After a moment's pause I said, "Pat, that guy was me." Disguised as I was in my costume and makeup, Pat hadn't recognized me.

After weeks of recuperation Pat started coming to worship at our church. A little while later he joined my Sunday-school class. That continued for a couple of years until one day he yelled across the street, "Hey, come over here. I need to tell you something."

He told me he had been asked to become a deacon in our church of over two thousand members. It seems incredible how far God had brought this guy. For years he'd lived a life without God having any meaningful part in it. Now God had moved Pat all the way to where he'd become a faithful Christian and a leader in our church. I remain amazed that God could reveal Himself even by using my sinful weakness and failing.

God Is Patient

A Mustard Seed of Trust

Lynn Ludwick

*A*nd they lived happily ever after.

I'd been raised on fairy tales and Broadway musicals, conditioned to expect that marriage would fill my deepest yearnings. My goal in life was to be a wife and mother. I waited for that "someday" when my Prince Charming would ride into town on his white horse and become the chief supplier of my happiness.

The man of my dreams did come along and capture my heart. We pledged our love to each other and vowed to live God-honoring lives. Shortly after we married, however, my husband's work schedule kept him away from church on Sundays. I soon fell into the careless habit of staying away as well. Before long we bought into the counterculture and drifted into an all-inclusive spirituality—a whatever-works-for-you philosophy. I relegated God to somewhere out there in the cosmos.

I occasionally prayed for important things such as a family, for we'd been told we'd be unable to have children. However, when our daughter was born, I thought it nice of God to answer my need. Soon, three little ones romped through our home.

I had achieved my goal in life, certain that I would enjoy the storybook ending. My marriage was solid, and I was a model homemaker. I cooked from scratch, sewed, decorated our home with creative skill, and canned garden produce. At last I was truly happy. I didn't need God and seldom thought about Him.

Then cracks in my marriage became visible. My husband and I talked less and less, and he grew emotionally distant. I became depressed. I tried to be a better wife, to pull things together, but to no avail. We had veered seriously off course and teetered on the brink, but I just knew we could fix things. Somehow we would be okay once more.

At one point I asked my husband, "What's wrong?"

I was totally unprepared for his answer. Though all his words killed my hopes and dreams that evening, one sentence punctured my heart, "I just don't love you anymore."

When we had said "I do" thirteen years earlier, I never doubted that only death would part us. But now we were apart. The day my husband backed out of our driveway for the last time, half my heart left with him, shattering the oneness we once shared.

He had chosen a new path in life, and I was set aside, left to cope with overwhelming devastation. And left to help our young children understand what I grappled with myself—why Daddy no longer came home at night.

I didn't need God and seldom thought about Him.

I took a few tentative steps toward God, thinking perhaps I needed Him after all. With a shaky and self-centered reborn faith, I begged God to bring my husband home. I longed to restore the perfect life I thought we'd had. Nothing else would do.

As the weeks passed, I posed a million what-if questions and wept gallons of tears. I constantly telephoned friends, seeking consolation they could not give, though they listened and offered their love. My world narrowed until it centered on a single focal point—pain. A pain so real it became physical. I could barely eat and slogged through each day in a dreary daze.

God Is Deliverer

Moment by moment, hour by hour, my husband's words tore at what was left of my heart. Then one day, as I drove a country road on a late summer afternoon, the condemning sentence reached a crescendo. *"I just don't love you anymore."* Tears of unbearable grief overwhelmed me. The tattered threads of hope that held me together unraveled, and my world collapsed. I could not go on.

Just ahead I saw my escape: a massive Douglas fir standing at the edge of the small forest I was skirting. The road curved, but I kept driving straight. In a moment I would die and be set free.

> The day my husband backed out of our driveway for the last time, half my heart left with him.

I gunned the engine, and my car surged forward. When the tires ground into the gravel shoulder, the car jerked and I fought for control. Rocks clanged against the wheels. And yet I still plunged forward. I had only one thought—to end my pain.

The distance closed, and the tree loomed as an unyielding wall, its boughs like beckoning arms waiting to embrace me. My mind faded to darkness, totally devoid of light. I veered off the road, and the crunch of rocks yielded to the hard forest floor.

Then God spoke.

With a wordless message, He penetrated my shattered heart. Against the black backdrop of my mind, I saw my three children. Their faces shone, their blond hair sparkled as if backlit with sunshine. Each freckle stood out. I could almost hear their soft whispers, *"I love you, Mommy."*

Small vignettes seemed to play before my eyes—scenes of what lay ahead for these innocent little ones. Scenes of what I would miss if I continued my course: In a couple of weeks my six-year-old daughter would climb the steps onto the big yellow bus and head to first grade, but I wouldn't be there to hand her the new lunch pail we'd chosen together. In a few years my four-year-old son would kick his first soccer goal and look to the cheering crowd, but I would be absent. And I wouldn't be there to punch holes in the lid of a jar that held all the bugs he collected. And the baby, my one-year-old, still needed someone to carry him and change his diapers. He was a cuddler and dispensed slurpy kisses that melted my heart. I would miss his first steps and the funny words he'd utter in his toddler years.

You would abandon your children?

"NO!" I shrieked and jammed on the brakes. I yanked hard on the wheel and pulled back toward the road. The car swerved as I slowed on the shoulder. "God! No, no!" My sweaty hands shook so violently I could barely grasp the steering wheel. I brought the car to a stop, then cut the engine and leaned the seat back.

Who do you trust?

"Not You, God," I whispered. I'd made my marriage my highest priority, and when it failed, there was nothing left. My despair had grown, eventually shutting out everything else, even my children. Yes, I could have found my release and ended my pain, but I would have left my children a legacy of never-ending pain.

Yet God loved me enough to rescue me. He had reached into my crumbled soul and reminded me how much my children needed me. My tears of anguish turned to tears of relief.

With only a tiny glimmer of hope and a mustard seed of trust, I chose life—until the time when *He* decides to call me home. Trusting God mattered. It was all that mattered.

God Is Deliverer

God Is Everlasting

THE BREAKFAST ANGEL

Gay Sorensen

Early on a warm September morning several years ago, I was sitting at the kitchen table gloomily sipping coffee, pondering the fact that our cupboards and refrigerator were bare and wondering where our next meal would come from.

Just home from a monthlong hospital stay, I was recently divorced and had lost my job as a secretary in a small architectural firm as a result of my illness. By now we had run out of food and money. I had prayed the night before that the Lord would help us in our financial crisis.

Then we heard a knock at the front door. When my fifteen-year-old daughter opened it, there stood her best friend, Codie. Mary Beth invited Codie to come in, and as Codie bounded into the kitchen, she announced cheerily, "Mornin' Gay! I'm sharing breakfast with you this morning."

She put down the bag she had carried and unpacked a can of frozen orange juice, eggs, and bread. Amazed and almost speechless, I wondered, *does God answer prayers this quickly?* I was sure that we hadn't confided about our plight to anyone. How could she have known?

"Oh, Codie, thank you honey, you're an angel," I said as I hugged her. "I don't know how you knew, but we were out of food, and this is an answer to prayer."

"I didn't know that," she said. "I just felt like I wanted to bring this to you."

I had become a Christian two months before my illness struck, and in our current crisis I had wondered if God had abandoned us. Now my faith was being restored and strengthened as never before—just by this one little act of kindness when we needed it most. It was a little miracle! I was astounded that God had answered my prayer so quickly.

But little did I know what further "little miracles" God had in store for us. And I didn't know then that I faced an extended six-month period of recuperation.

Almost immediately after being released from the hospital, I had filed a claim for disability insurance, but was told there would be a long waiting period before it would start. I had two teenagers to support. And I was concerned over how I would take care of my family financially until the disability checks began to arrive.

In the afternoon of the same day that our "breakfast angel" appeared on the doorstep, we had a second visitor. It was another "angel" in the person of Cindy.

Cindy and Frank were a young couple from our church. They lived nearby, and Mary Beth often babysat for their two little girls. Cindy said, "Frank and I have talked it over, and we feel that God wants us to give you our tithe money this month."

She handed me a sizeable check. Again, I was astounded as I tearfully thanked her. This was another answer to my prayer of the night before. I could hardly believe it—two answers in less than twenty-four hours!

We went to the supermarket, and after we restocked our shelves and refrigerator, I carefully made out a budget to see how long our gift from the Lord would last. Not long, I guessed. And the rent was due soon. But bolstered by those two answers to prayer, I resolved not to worry. Instead, I thanked God for what we had received. I felt at

God Is Everlasting

peace with a confidence that the good Lord would meet our needs as they arose.

A few days before our October rent was due, I called the owner of our apartment building and explained our situation. I told him that I didn't know how or when we would be able to come up with the rent payment, but that I was sure we would get it to him. He told me not to worry.

A day or so later, he called and reminded me that several months earlier I had recarpeted the living room at my own expense with the understanding that I could take the carpeting with me when I moved. He offered us a month's free rent if I would leave the carpet in place. This was a solution I hadn't thought of, and I knew that this had to be yet another answer to prayer.

The unexpected was becoming the expected.

The first of October came and went. The rent had been taken care of, but soon we ran out of money again. By now, the unexpected was becoming the expected, so I wasn't as surprised at the next event as I would have been if all the other "little miracles" hadn't occurred in such rapid succession.

Yes, the doorbell rang again at the most opportune time—just at the end of the money. This time it was George, my ex-husband. "I had a feeling you could use some extra money this month," he explained as he handed me not only a check for the monthly child support, but an extra two hundred dollars.

I was speechless! This was completely out of character for him in those days.

That week I carefully doled out the money for utility bills, food for the family, and other necessities. The money lasted exactly until the arrival of my first disability check.

Six months after coming home from the hospital, I had totally recovered and was ready to go back to work. I prayed again—this time for a new job. I prayed not only for a job, but for just the right one. Within a short time I found a position in another architectural firm, with a Christian architect as my new boss, an unexpected blessing. It turned out to be the best job of my career, and he became the nicest boss I ever had. I worked for him for eight years.

When that difficult period of our lives ended, I looked back on it as an exciting adventure. God had completely taken care of us, and He had given me the gift of faith. With that, I realized how much God really loved me, cared about my every need, and was there to help me with all the details of my life.

I've lived through some tough times through the years since then. But I have found that the Lord has never failed to provide for my every need. I knew then, as I know now, that God hears and answers prayers. And I thank Him with all my heart for not only His gift of provision, but for His gift of faith. And it all began with that simple little act of kindness, given to us by a "breakfast angel."

God Is Everlasting

God Is Forgiving

THE FIRE OF GOD'S LOVE

Laurie Vines

When I was thirteen, a fire devastated my life.

I still remember the brilliant idea that led to the destruction. While cooking in my family's kitchen, I thought of a marvelous prank. My best friend, Amy, had asked me to call her and wake her up, but I wanted to sneak into her house and scare her instead. She only lived a block away, so I dropped everything and ran down the street to surprise her.

I could barely wait to see the look on her face.

Amy's parents were still at work like mine were, and I knew where her family hid the spare key. I tiptoed quietly into her room and yelled her name. She sat straight up and screamed. We laughed all the way from her bedroom to the living room.

Minutes later someone interrupted our talking and laughter with loud knocks. When we opened the front door and saw my brother, Troy, we knew that something bad had happened. He quickly told me the house was on fire.

While running down the road, it dawned on me what had happened. All my emotions sank deep inside of me when I saw the fireman putting out the fire I had caused. I had not turned off the pot of grease for my french fries when I left to scare Amy, and our house stood covered in smoke and soot. Dread took hold of me.

I expected a look of disappointment or anger from my dad when he arrived. Instead, I only noticed his sad and worried face. He walked straight up to me and hugged me. My mother did the same when she arrived. My older brother encouraged me with his loving smile, but I cannot remember my older sister Lisa's reaction. I do remember feeling covered in guilt.

After staying in a hotel for a brief period, we moved into an apartment weeks before Christmas. Shortly after Christmas, I caught a bad case of strep throat and mononucleosis and slept endlessly. Normally I would have been excited about the holidays, but not that year. I did not want to do anything or go anywhere, even when I got better. I did not care about much, but I did notice my sister seemed more distant than before the fire.

Lisa was a senior in high school and proudly wore her boyfriend's letterman jacket. She was a cheerleader and had been accepted into a very good college. Each time I saw her walk into our shared bedroom, I felt as though she resented not having a normal senior year and living in that small apartment. And I knew it was my fault.

Lisa never said much about the fire. No one did. During those months in the apartment, I was sheltered from any discussion about what happened. I never heard about how, financially, it hurt my parents, or about the keepsakes that could never be replaced.

I never heard about the strain of moving from our house right before Christmas or all of the decisions my parents had to make. But nonetheless I knew, and layers of regret and insecurity formed deep inside of me.

Knowing how everything affected me, my friend Amy reached out to me. She invited me to church. She introduced me to a wonderful group of young believers, and because of her, I accepted Christ into my life. I experienced joy and gladness for the first time in months, but I could never seem to wipe away my insecurities. I strayed away from

God Is Forgiving

my faith and allowed my life to get more and more out of control. Finally, halfway through my college years it hit me: I had nowhere else to turn but back to God.

At age nineteen I wholeheartedly dedicated my life to knowing and serving God. Then I began to discover, for the first time, my worth apart from my insecurities and my mistakes. God stirred desires within my heart. I purposed to get everything right that I could in my life—including being healed from the fire.

At a family gathering one day, my sister sat in the kitchen alone. I joined her, and we started to talk about how we were doing. I took the

> Layers of regret and insecurity
> formed deep inside of me.

plunge and told her that I had been thinking about the fire. I asked her if she would forgive me for any pain that I caused. She said that she never blamed me for anything. She told me that my mom, my dad, and my brother all said they wished it had been them who caused the fire instead of me. At that moment I realized they never discussed the fire because they wanted to protect me, not because they were angry with me. At last, I no longer felt that looming sense of regret and guilt.

I also realized how God was with us during that time. My brother, Troy, and I were both home that day. When I left the house to surprise Amy, he slept soundly in his room. He never heard the fire alarm, but he woke up anyway. After smelling the smoke and seeing that the kitchen curtains were on fire, he got out and went to a neighbor's house to call 911. He then ran down the street to tell Amy and me. I never left a note saying where I was; Troy just knew. God kept my brother alive, waking him at just the right time and keeping me from unthinkable regret.

I remembered the flood of help and encouragement that God brought. Our neighbors collected money, and attaching it to a small Christmas tree, they handed it to my parents to help us through the season. I went back and thanked Amy's family for all of their support and shared how their faith had a major impact on my life.

I also learned that the entire high school faculty met to discuss what had happened. They came up with ways to give us three teenagers the love and support we needed. No wonder my teachers were so nice that year!

Yes, God's hand guided us then, but it took time and a healed heart to see that clearly. When my fiancé, Russell, told me that he wanted to be a fireman, I could accept it. My heart had been healed of my past. For five years Russell enjoyed a firefighting career, and he never suffered any serious injury. Once more God revealed His hand through the fire and taught me to trust in His goodness.

I am convinced that I cannot escape future fiery trials. But when I smell the smoke of tough times, I pay special attention to what is carrying me—God's love.

His love always withstands the fire. It can never, ever be burned away.

God Is Forgiving

Uncle Charlie's Visit

James H. Smith, as told to Leslie Payne

In 1924 I was born a nobody—a baby boy born to an unwed teenage girl in Baltimore City. A baby boy passed around for the first ten months of life until my great-uncle Charlie and great-aunt Ola took me in. In a neighborhood known as Sandtown, I grew up with Uncle Charlie and Aunt Ola, took on their name, and enjoyed their love. Yet I grew up not knowing who I was and thought I was a nobody.

Uncle Charlie thought differently. So did God.

Uncle Charlie was a strong man who worked as a hod carrier. A hod was a three-sided wooden box with a long handle, piled with bricks or cement. Uncle Charlie lifted the fully loaded hod over his shoulder and climbed a ladder up the side of a building to deliver his load to the skilled masonry workers. He did it again and again, all day long. As my uncle worked to provide for his family, his body was shaped by menial labor.

My life was shaped by his.

When I was old enough, Uncle Charlie and I built a wagon from scrap wood, using the wheels from an old baby carriage. Barely big enough to swing a hammer, I became the proud owner of my own wagon. Uncle Charlie nicknamed me "The Wagon Master" and taught me to use the wagon with purpose.

I felt grown up as I set out to use my wagon to add to the family finances. Pulling the wagon behind me, I walked to the neighborhood market, loaded up folks' groceries, and delivered the food to their homes. Most of the time, they tipped me with a penny or two. I covered many miles as I pulled my little wagon behind me. With the jingle of change in my pocket, I began to feel I was better than a nobody. I was helping provide for the family, just like Uncle Charlie.

There were six kids in Uncle Charlie's house, yet I was the only one who was a blood relation. He had a big heart and loved children. Like me, the others had no other place to go. Uncle Charlie and Aunt Ola took us all into their house and gave us a home. They loved and disciplined us as if we were their own flesh and blood. In return, we each did what we could to help out when money was scarce, which was most of the time.

With Uncle Charlie's pay as a hod carrier and the nickels and dimes the rest of us earned, we got by. He kept us warm; he kept us fed; and if we got sick, he was there by our side to care for us. He often used a salve or liquid to treat a cough or cold. Whenever I was sick, he'd approach me with a bottle in one hand and a spoon in the other. I knew there was no use protesting the bitter taste of his treatments. Eventually my mouth opened and the spoon went in—it was another expression of my uncle's love.

My great-uncle was a man of moral character and wanted us to be the best we could be, so he pushed us kids. We all worked hard at home, scrubbing floors and polishing our marble doorsteps, a source of Baltimore pride. He made sure we were in church every Sunday where I served as an altar boy. And he put me in Boy Scouts as soon as I was old enough.

Times were difficult for us during the Great Depression, but he never accepted any government handouts. My proud uncle did not believe in welfare, no matter how many patches we had on our pants.

God Is Majestic

He said he was man enough to make a way for his family, and he always did.

Uncle Charlie was also a man of prayer.

"I pray for you just like I pray for myself," he'd say, as he looked me in the eye. "But I pray for you even more."

He told me that someday I might be a real somebody. The way he said it made me want it.

As the years marched by, Uncle Charlie started using a cane, and I made my own way in the world. Toward the end of World War II, I dropped out of high school and served in the merchant marines. When I returned home to Baltimore, I got up the nerve to ask Louise Blount to marry me. We didn't have much except love, so Uncle Charlie made room for us in his house. We married on October 1, 1946, at the preacher's house. After a reception of cookies and Kool-Aid, we walked home to Uncle Charlie's to start our married life.

We set off to make a home of our own when we began to have children. Soon we had three beautiful daughters close together, just like stair steps. I was a husband and a father, working hard to prove myself as I provided for my family. I was trying to be a somebody.

As he walked through the house, his cane tapped rhythmically against the floorboards.

Aunt Ola died, and Uncle Charlie was up in years, so he moved in with us. My girls adored his attention, little games, and wise ways. It had been years since Uncle Charlie raised me, but his love for children was still strong. As he walked through the house, his cane tapped rhythmically against the floorboards, blending with the sound of the girls' giggles and tears. Those family sounds were like a song I loved to hear over and over.

When he was ninety-six years old, Uncle Charlie's cane was propped up in the corner of his room for the last time. The man who had worked so hard to fill the void in my life died. The questions of my own self-worth lived on. Uncle Charlie was gone. I could no longer look to him for wisdom and advice.

The Lord knew my needs. In His perfect time, He gave the direction I needed that changed the course of my life.

A number of years after Uncle Charlie passed on, I became sick with double pneumonia for the second time. It's bad enough the first time, but it's even worse the second. Louise did her best to care for me as I lay in our bed growing weaker each day. Beads of perspiration trickled down my forehead, and my body ached with fever. I labored with each breath. Family and friends prayed for me, not knowing if I would survive.

One day the familiar sound of tapping against the wood floor caused me to rally my strength and open my eyes. I knew the sound of Uncle Charlie's cane as well as I knew the sound of my own voice. Though I was puzzled as to how he got into the room, I was eager to look into the face of my hero.

There he stood beside my bed with a bottle in one hand and a spoon in the other, exactly like when I was a little boy. He poured liquid from the bottle into the spoon and put it in my mouth.

As the warm fluid slid down my throat, he said, *"The Lord's going to use you. Now preach, go preach my God."*

"But I'm not prepared."

"You will be."

I was too worn out from fever to protest, but I tried to look into his face as he straightened up. His clothes were bright white and wrapped around him like a robe. I felt peaceful as I enjoyed his presence. Too soon, his cane tapped in rhythm against the floor as he turned and walked away from me, and then he disappeared.

God Is Majestic

From the moment of Uncle Charlie's visit, I got better. Here I am today more than fifty years later, a retired United Methodist pastor. That visit from Uncle Charlie was my call to the ministry, the answer to so many of my questions. Uncle Charlie had been dead for years, yet the Lord still used the man in my life. Folks ask me if it was a dream or a vision. Best answer I can them give is, "It was Uncle Charlie."

Since that visit I've completed my GED, seminary training, and countless continuing-education credits from colleges and seminaries. I've pastored congregations, served on mission trips, and traveled the world. Maryland governors, mayors, and members of Congress have presented me with awards and citations. I've even been awarded an honorary doctorate degree.

As nice as all those accomplishments have been, none of them made me a somebody. You see, I was *always* somebody with a purpose because I was one of God's children. As I pursued the purpose God had for me, the pieces of my life came together, the emptiness was filled, and I realized my own worth.

Since the moment God created me, I was somebody important in His eyes simply because He loved me. Uncle Charlie knew that, and finally I did too.

God Is Sovereign

THE BEST BIRTHDAY GIFT EVER

Renae Brumbaugh

"*If* you don't choose a place soon, I'm stopping at *the next* place I see!" Dad growled from behind the steering wheel. We were whizzing down Houston's North Freeway, and there were just too many restaurants to choose from.

Mother and I laughed. For as long as we could remember, it had been the same. Dad usually wanted one of us to choose a restaurant, and we could never make up our minds. He always ended up threatening to stop at *the next* place, and he often did. We had eaten at some pretty interesting establishments over the years.

But today was special. It was our birthday. Mom and I enjoyed sharing the same birthday, and Dad was taking us to the restaurant of our choice to celebrate. I had come home from college for this dinner. We'd spent every one of my twenty-one birthdays together, and I cherished the tradition.

Mom looked at me and smiled. "How about Mexican food?"

I grimaced. "I'm not in the mood for anything spicy tonight. What about steak?"

"No, there's not a good steak place around here. We'd have to drive clear across town. Let's see . . . how about Chinese?"

Before we knew it, Dad was pulling off the highway and into the parking lot of Luby's Cafeteria. Mom and I groaned in unison.

"Dad, we eat here all the time!"

He smiled at me and said, "You had your chance. Besides, we've been driving around for nearly an hour, and I'm starved."

Mom and I grumbled and got out of the car. This was not exactly the glamorous evening we'd had in mind when we'd dressed in our silk blouses and high-heeled shoes. Oh, well. At least we could choose what we wanted to eat.

We filed in line, got our trays, and made our choices. Dad and I both chose my favorite—chicken-fried steak smothered in gravy, with mashed potatoes on the side. Mom got baked cod. We each selected a different dessert, with plans to sample each one.

Dad led the way to our table, and we unloaded our trays. After the "Amen" was said, Mom and I jumped right into conversation, while Dad jumped right into his meal. Mom asked about school and friends and my classes, and I asked about her job and the neighbors and Beau, the family dog. Somewhere in there, I realized I needed to go to the ladies' room.

"I'll be right back."

Mom and Dad smiled at me. I was so grateful to have my parents. Through the years, my brother and I had watched them make a difference in so many lives. They were the kind of people who never met a stranger and who loved people genuinely. They had opened their home to people in need, had freely used their modest income to help others, and had openly shared their love for Christ and His love for all people. They had modeled for their children what it meant to live out your faith. I prayed that, like them, God would use me to share His love.

In the restroom, I washed my hands and thought of the Triple Chocolate Delight that was waiting for me, wondering if, now that I was a legal adult, I could get away with eating dessert first. Probably not. I could just hear Mom say, "Eat a few more bites of your vegetables, honey."

A woman entered with her adorable two-year-old daughter. The child was wearing a dainty dress and bright bows. I smiled at her. "What a pretty girl you have there!" I told the woman.

"Thank you," she said. "She's a handful!" Then, catching a glimpse of me in the mirror, she seemed surprised. She stared for a moment before looking back at her daughter.

I dried my hands and started to leave.

"Excuse me," the woman said. I turned, and she looked hesitant. "Never mind," she whispered.

I started to leave, and she called, "Miss, did you ever work at Randall's grocery store?"

> ## "Miss, did you ever work at
> ## Randall's grocery store?"

"Miss, did you ever work at Randall's grocery store?"

"Yes. I was a cashier there during high school," I replied, smiling at the memory. That had been some backaching work.

"I thought I recognized you . . ." She looked thoughtful.

I smiled and turned once again.

"Miss, I need to tell you something."

I turned to face her, confused at this odd interaction. "Yes?" I replied, a little nervously. What could this stranger possibly need to tell me? Did I have lipstick on my teeth or toilet paper caught on my shoe?

She looked at the floor. "It may seem strange for me to tell you this, but I used to be really messed up. My life was a train wreck, and I was into all sorts of awful things. I was angry and hurt. I used to come through your line at Randall's, and you were nice to me. One day, you invited me to your church. I still remember . . . Bethel Baptist, right?"

Wide-eyed, I nodded.

God Is Sovereign

"You didn't judge me. You told me Jesus loved me and wanted to change my life. I listened to what you said, and I knew I needed to make some changes. I never went to your church, but I did go to another church. I accepted Christ, and He has truly changed my life." She paused and looked into my eyes. "I just wanted to say thank you."

I was stunned. I finally choked out, "Ma'am, that's wonderful. You don't know how much that means to me. You see, today is my birthday, and you've just given me the best birthday gift I could ask for."

"Happy birthday!" she exclaimed. We both laughed, and then we hugged. Her daughter needed her attention, so we shared a few more words and smiles, and I left.

Dazed, I walked back through the crowded restaurant. I didn't remember meeting this woman. But I did remember praying each day before going to work that God would use me in someone's life. You'd be surprised at what people will tell a grocery-store clerk, and I had shared Christ with many people. I found our table and sat down.

"We were starting to worry," Mom said.

I smiled. "God just gave me a birthday present." I went on to tell Mom and Dad what had just happened. They were stunned, amazed, and deeply touched. I think they had received a gift too.

I never saw the woman again, but I have never forgotten her. She was God's reminder to me that He is personally involved in our lives. In all of His infinite glory, He had given me a wonderful gift—and on my birthday. Of all the places we could have eaten that night, He directed us to Luby's. And of all the times I could have gone to the ladies' room, He took me there at precisely the right moment. He allowed me to see a glimpse of the difference we can make in people's lives without even knowing it, if we are faithful to share His love.

It was the best birthday gift I've ever received.

God Is Good

BY DIVINE APPOINTMENT

Susan Kelly Skitt

"*I*s that your son?" I asked as I slid my salad container onto the table and turned to the blonde woman standing next to me.

"Yes," she replied.

"He's very kind to help my son," I said.

My three-year-old son, Joel, had been struggling to play a race-car video game mounted on a stand in the fast-food restaurant, when this older boy stepped in to help. While the kids played, we remarked how we both had exercise clothes on and chatted about the different gyms we attended. Soon the conversation turned back to our children.

"Do you have any other children?"

"Yes," I replied. "I have another son."

"How old?"

"Thirteen."

"Wow, that's a big age difference." The woman looked at my son and then at me. "Is this your second marriage?"

I felt as if someone had pierced my heart with an arrow. *Well, God, do I tell this woman what happened?* Sometimes I didn't mind talking about it, but other times it hurt too much.

"Yes, it is." I shifted from one foot to the other, clutching my car keys. "My first husband died in a car accident when my son was nine months old. I remarried a few years later."

"Wow . . . that must have been very painful," the woman said, sympathetic distress filling her eyes.

"Yes. It was." After pausing for a moment, I added, "But there is something more painful than death."

Her eyes grew wide. "What?"

"Going into eternity without God."

Where did that come from, Lord? While often bold in my witness for Christ, I certainly had never said that before.

The woman swallowed and glanced toward the door. I wanted to say more but didn't. A few moments later, we exchanged good-byes, and I watched as the two walked into the parking lot and out of my life.

There is something more painful than death.

The next day, I picked up my son from the bus stop after school, planning to take the kids to the gym where I worked out.

"Hi, hon, did you have a good day at school?"

"Yep." Jared tossed his backpack into the car.

I gazed out the car window at the clear blue sky, and suddenly an idea popped into my head. "You know what, guys? It's sunny today. Let's skip the gym and get some exercise outside. Let's go to the park."

"Yea! Can we go to the playground?" Joel clutched his soccer ball and bounced up and down in his car seat.

"Sure, and we can take a walk next to the lake, and you can kick your soccer ball."

"Sounds good, Mom." Jared took a swig from his water bottle and hopped into the front seat. "Let's go."

For some reason, I decided to park our car near the old playground at the far end of a local park. Most families usually took their children to the new playground in a less-isolated area. But with my teenage son, who was the size of a football player, I felt pretty safe going to this remote area surrounded by woods.

After a short walk by the lake, we trudged up the narrow path to the playground. I plopped onto a park bench while Jared pushed Joel on a rusted, chain-link swing. A warm spring breeze rustled the leaves on the trees. I closed my eyes, enjoying the peace and quiet.

Minutes later, the silence was broken by the squeaking of a child's bicycle wheels on the path behind me. I heard the voices of a man and woman and smiled in greeting as the family walked into view.

I stared at the blonde-haired woman and boy in front of me. We both started talking at once.

"Didn't you . . ."

"Aren't you the one . . . ?"

We both shook our heads and chuckled. "We saw each other at lunch yesterday," we explained to the man.

I felt goose bumps on my arms. *Lord, this is too weird. Out of all the places and times to see this woman again—you must have arranged this appointment. Help me say what you want me to say.*

"This is my husband," the woman said.

"It's nice to meet you." I stood and shook each of their hands.

"We just got back from his nephew's funeral and decided we needed to come to the park. His nephew died in his twenties like your first husband."

Our boys began playing together on an old wooden structure that crisscrossed in L-shaped patterns. The beams stepped up in elevation with several single-beam bridges to cross like balance beams. It was difficult for my three-year-old to climb, but he was determined to follow the older boy's lead.

We continued to chat about our families, when she told me about

God Is Good

how years ago, her sister's son also died while in his twenties. Her sister had been active in church but stopped going when her son died.

She looked at me, her blue eyes misty. "She lost her faith in God."

I didn't know what to say but felt compelled to tell her about my faith. "Even though it's been painful for me, Jesus Christ is my personal Savior. My husband knew Jesus as his personal Savior too. I know I will see him again one day in heaven. I can trust God because Jesus died and rose again to give us life. That's how much He loves us."

We continued talking about life and God. The woman told me how, after the death of her two nephews, she'd struggled with believing God really cares about people.

As we talked, I noticed my younger son trying to follow his new friend across a single wooden beam about four feet off the ground. All at once my son's foot slipped. My new friend, who was standing closer to the beam, quickly extended her hand to save my son from falling. Joel grasped her hand for dear life and safely crossed the rest of the way.

I put my hand over my rapidly beating heart. "Thank you."

We stopped talking for a few minutes until I felt compelled to break the silence.

"You know, just like you helped my son, God wants to help us. He wants to save us for all eternity. You reached out your hand, and my son grabbed it. God is reaching out his hand to us, and all we need to do is grab it. He won't ever let us go."

We stood watching our children play. My older son sat on a swing, pushing mulch around with his foot. I knew he had been listening to our conversation. I thought about how difficult it must be for him to hear me talk about his father's death through the years, and I silently prayed for God to meet his needs.

Shadows from the setting sun crawled across the playground. I called to my three-year-old, "It's getting late, Joel. We need to go home."

With a final farewell to the other family, I walked down the winding path with my sons. Joel ran ahead, kicking his soccer ball, and Jared draped his arm across my shoulders. When we neared the parking lot, I told Jared about how I had met the woman the day before and about our conversation.

"Wow, Mom. It's like God brought you two together for a reason."

"I know, Jared. I believe this was a divine appointment that God set up."

I smiled at my sons and thought about how I have seen God work time and time again, filling my life with so many blessings.

God's guiding hand has been with me all the way, through the good and the bad, the happy and the sad. Psalm 31:15 says, "My future is in your hands."

I can think of no other appointment I'd rather keep than the one that God arranges.

God Is Good

God Is Shield

THE SHADOW OF HIS WINGS

Pat Stockett Johnston

*S*omething's wrong. Why else would I wake up at three a.m.?

I heard explosions in the distant, downtown area of Beirut, where my husband and I were missionaries. Nothing new about that nightly serenade, for at the time, in 1975, Palestinians and Lebanese Muslims and Christians were engaged in their fifth month of civil war.

Wait. My nightgown feels wet. And I just felt the baby move. Oh, no! That's not the baby. That's contractions. I'm only six months pregnant. It's too early for the baby to be born!

I shook Gordon awake. "The baby's coming. You have to drive me to the hospital right now."

"Can you wait until the curfew ends at six a.m.?"

"I don't think so. I'll pack a bag while you go ask the neighbors to stay with the kids."

We climbed into our car a few minutes later and headed down Subtiyya Hill toward Hamra. Gordon patted my knee. "The fighters are on the lookout for men who are alone. I'll turn on the inside car lights, and I want you to sit up tall. Hopefully everyone will notice a woman's with me."

Our eyes searched for armed men along the road. "We'll face the most danger when we cross the Karentina Bridge," Gordon said grimly. "So many people have died trying to cross it. Let's hope the snipers are asleep."

We approached the bridge in silence. After successfully crossing it without incident, Gordon whispered, "It's a miracle. No men, no weapons in sight."

At the hospital Gordon waited to hear the doctor's report. "She needs to be admitted for a few days," the doctor explained.

My husband kissed my check. "I can't wait any longer," he said. "I've got to get back to the kids before heavy fighting breaks out again." Thirty minutes later he called to say he'd arrived home safely.

Those four days alone in a maternity waiting room dragged by. Finally the doctor said, "You will be released tomorrow morning. But you need to stay near the hospital until the baby is born."

The next day Gordon made plans. "The Trimbles have invited you to stay with them. The kids and I will come to Hamra as soon as it's safe. I'll hunt for a furnished apartment near the hospital."

One week later our family was reunited in a rented seventh-floor apartment near the University of Beirut Hospital. The army tank parked at the intersection below us, however, didn't make us feel secure. How long would we live here?

A truce agreement was reached and held until the end of September. We enjoyed two quiet weeks: we were free to go up and down the stairs, the kids went to school and back, we had dinner together in the evenings, and Beverly and Keith did homework. Then one night it started again. Machine-gun fire. The blasts of bazooka rockets destroying buildings in downtown Beirut. Tracer bullets lit the sky. Sirens blared and tires squealed as ambulances raced to the hospital.

The next morning I glanced down from the balcony at the street. "The stores have their steel doors and shutters closed," I announced. "School won't be in session today."

"Let's catch the news," Gordon said as he tuned the radio to the BBC.

That's when we heard the announcement: "The fifty-sixth truce in the Lebanese Civil War has been broken. Gunmen are again shooting

God Is Shield

at each other from the Holiday Inn and the Intercontinental Hotel. Fighting is heavy along the Green Line that divides the city between east and west. Gunfire can be heard coming from the Borj. All schools, businesses, and government offices are closed. The Department of State has instructed the United States Embassy in Beirut to evacuate all unnecessary personnel immediately. American civilians should leave Lebanon as soon as possible."

Everything closed? Evacuation? What would happen to us?

Gordon spent a lot of time on the phone that day. After dinner, during our family devotion time, he shared the news with our children. "I spoke with Mommy's doctor. He said it wouldn't be safe for her to fly. He says we should stay here in Hamra until after the baby is born in December. He warned that, if we fly, the baby might be born before it's developed enough to survive. I think we all want a healthy baby brother or sister, don't we?"

Our three children nodded their heads.

> "Let's ask God to make it possible for Mommy to go to the hospital during the day."

"God helped us find this apartment. And He can keep us safe the next few weeks. We can trust Him to meet our every need."

A few days before Thanksgiving, the BBC announced that the Lebanese government had set a curfew again. During devotions that night, Gordon explained the curfew to the children. Then he sighed.

"This creates a real problem for us. Mommy might need to go to the hospital in the middle of the night. Not even the doctor can control when a baby is born," he said to the children.

Beverly had an idea. "Let's ask God to make it possible for Mommy to go to the hospital during the day."

"Please God! Make it a daytime trip," was Beverly's nightly prayer from then on.

About three o'clock on the Wednesday afternoon before Thanksgiving, I felt the baby move. "It doesn't feel like it's just stretching," I told Gordon. "I think we'd better get to the hospital."

Gordon hollered, "Grab your jackets, kids. The baby is on its way!"

We dropped our children off at the home of our friends, the Harts. On the way Beverly said, "God heard our prayers. Mommy's going to the hospital in the afternoon."

When Gordon returned to the Harts' house to pick up the children that afternoon, I wasn't with him.

"What happened? Is something wrong? Where's Mommy?" The children's voices were full of concern.

"Don't worry. The doctor said Mommy was ready to have the baby. But at five o'clock she told me not to wait any longer. She asked me to get you kids home before the evening curfew."

"How will we know when the baby has been born?" asked Beverly. "How will we know if we have a baby brother or a baby sister?"

"I'll call the hospital to check on Mommy and the baby," Gordon told her.

Gordon called the hospital at seven o'clock. No baby. He called before he put the children to bed at eight. No baby. He called at nine, ten, and eleven. The baby still hadn't been born. The operator at the hospital told him no one would answer the phones after midnight because of staffing problems.

At eight o'clock on Thursday morning my family finally learned that baby Craig had been born at 12:30 a.m. on Thanksgiving Day.

"I think Mommy and baby Craig should be released from the hospital next week," Gordon told the children.

The next morning Gordon dropped off the kids and rushed to the hospital. Someone in the elevator said, "Did you hear what happened last night? Bullets flew into a patient's room."

God Is Shield

As Gordon continued to the nursery, he determined to get Craig and me out of the hospital as soon as possible. At the nursery, Gordon looked through the nursery-room window. Each bassinette had a name taped to it. A nurse asked, "Can I help you?"

"I'm looking for my son—baby Johnston."

His heart sank at her answer. "Mr. Johnston, your son's in the newborn intensive care unit. You need to talk to the doctor about his condition."

Gordon spotted baby Johnston lying in the NICU in an incubator with a tube up his nose. His voice trembled as he asked the doctor, "What's wrong with my son?"

"He's been diagnosed with pneumonia. We don't think it's life-threatening, and we plan to release him in about ten days."

I started to cry when Gordon entered my room. "Do you know about Craig? I just found out a little while ago that something was wrong. I haven't even seen him yet!"

"You've given me a beautiful new son," Gordon reassured me. "He's gorgeous! He looks a lot like Keith did . . . lots of straight brown hair. It could be so much worse. Craig has been born in a hospital with the most modern, up-to-date equipment for treating infants. We can thank God that he is in such good hands."

In a few days I was released from the hospital. Baby Craig, however, was not yet allowed to leave. My first night in the apartment, I noticed the gas burner flame on the stove was turning yellow. "Gordon, I think we're running out of bottled gas. Where will we be able to find more?"

During peacetime, trucks full of bottled gas drove the streets of Beirut, honking their horns to announce their presence.

"We'll have to pray for a truck to drive by tomorrow," he replied.

As I stepped out of the apartment building on my way to cuddle and feed Craig the next morning, I noticed a truckful of bottled gas parked in front of the door.

"Are these bottles empty or full?" I eagerly asked the driver.

"Full."

"Please don't leave." I begged. "I want to buy a bottle. I'll go get my husband." The elevator seemed to take forever to carry me back to the seventh floor. "Come quickly," I told Gordon. "A truck of bottled gas is downstairs!"

The kids grinned from ear to ear as their dad rolled the full bottle of gas into the kitchen. Beverly declared, "God knows we need to eat hot meals!" We hoped that bottle of gas would last through our remaining time in Beirut.

On my drive home from visiting Craig on his twelfth day at the hospital, I noticed the gas gauge showed almost empty. I looked for gas stations all the way back to the apartment. Every one had a big sign stating No Gas by the gas pumps.

The next morning Gordon announced that he was going to try to find some gas for the car. Keith chimed in, "I want to go with you."

An hour later the two burst into the apartment. "You won't believe what happened," Gordon declared. "We spent an hour driving to every gas station I knew about. Finally I said, 'I give up!'

"'Wait a minute, Daddy. There's a gas station over there,' Keith said.

"'Yes, but it has that No Gas sign by the pumps like the rest,' I replied.

"'Except the door is open, and I can see a man inside,' Keith said.

"I pulled the car into the station next to the man sitting on a chair by the door. In the shadows behind him were five-gallon containers.

"'Can you sell me some gas?' I asked.

"'How much do you want?'

"'Ten gallons will be enough for now.'

"The man poured ten gallons of the gasoline into the car!"

"Thank you, God, for leading Daddy and Keith to the right place today," we prayed that night. "And please don't let us run out of gas before we get to the airport."

God Is Shield

A time of celebration arrived when Craig was sixteen days old. His vital signs had been normal for twenty-four hours, and he was released from the hospital.

When we arrived home with him, Beverly, Keith, and Joanne sat on the sofa, so excited they could hardly sit still. All three took turns holding baby Craig. Then Beverly asked, "When can we leave Beirut?"

"A few things have to be taken care of first," explained Gordon. "Craig has to have an official document declaring him to be a United States citizen. We need to purchase airline tickets for six. And we need to do something about our expired Lebanese residence permits. I'll get right to work on the details. I'm sure we'll be out of here before you know it!"

Gordon spent the afternoon getting Craig's name added to his passport and buying tickets to Milan, Italy—the only flight out of Beirut with six remaining seats. That meant we'd only eat two more meals in Beirut—dinner that night and breakfast the next day.

Our friends, the Harts, dropped by that evening to take our food supplies to their place. Before they left, Dr. Hart pulled Gordon aside. "How will you get to the airport tomorrow morning?"

"I'll drive and leave the car in the airport parking lot."

"I don't think you should do that," Dr. Hart said. "I feel like God has instructed me to take your family to the airport. Our station wagon is larger than yours. The luggage rack on top can hold some of the suitcases."

"I can't let you do that," Gordon responded. "You know the airport road isn't safe."

"I insist," Dr. Hart said. "My Arab neighbor has volunteered to go with us so I won't be alone on the return trip to Hamra."

Finally, Gordon agreed.

Everyone had a restless night. Soon the suitcases were lined up in a row in the hall. Then the phone rang. "Foreigners have just been kidnapped on the airport road. You can't fly out today," our friend Habib said.

"If we wait for the roads to be safe, we may never leave Beirut," I replied. "Thank you for caring. Please pray for our safety."

Soon Dr. Hart and his Arab friend, George, arrived to load everything and everybody into the station wagon. We were packed in tight. George suggested we take a back road to the airport, and Dr. Hart followed his directions.

As we made our way from the Mediterranean Sea to the top of a hill, we noticed a group of Lebanese soldiers blocking the road. Their rifles were pointed straight at Dr. Hart.

"You have to turn back," they ordered. "Armed fighters are blocking the road to the airport from here."

> "Foreigners have just been kidnapped on the airport road. You can't fly out today."

"Don't pay any attention to them," George said confidently. "Go around them and turn right."

Dr. Hart slowly drove around the corner. The soldiers shrugged their shoulders and lowered their weapons. We were through the checkpoint!

Suddenly, our worst fears became reality. Just around the corner at the bottom of the hill was a second group of armed men. They weren't in uniform. These were guerrilla fighters. Several were holding guns. A man with a rifle waved for us to stop, and I was petrified.

Oh, no! After all we have been through, are we going to be killed on the road to the airport? God, help us!

"Don't be afraid," said George encouragingly. "Let me do the talking."

He rolled down his window. "Hello, friends!" he called in Arabic

God Is Shield

to the leader of the gang. "Peace be with you. I'm taking some of my friends to the airport. Tell me, are the roads safe around here?"

"Perfectly safe," the armed man replied. "Be on your way."

I could breathe again. We drove through two more groups of armed men that morning. Each time George asked if the roads were clear. Each time the answer was yes. Finally we pulled into the airport departure entrance.

Dr. Hart and George helped unload the luggage. Then Gordon explained, "We have one more obstacle before we can leave. Our expired Lebanese residence permits need to be extended."

George wasn't concerned. "I'll help you do that," he said cheerfully. "Let's ask directions to the Office of Immigration."

Finally Gordon and George returned to where the children, Dr. Hart, and I were sitting. "Well, can we leave?" I asked fearfully.

"We sure can!" Gordon said. "George was like an angel in disguise. With his help we got our residence permits extended. The immigration officer was so friendly I thought he was an old friend of George's. But I found out afterward that George had never met him before.

"I thanked George for what he did to help us—people he doesn't even know—get to the airport. George told me God had made getting people to the airport his special ministry during this time of war. That's why he was so willing to help."

After changing planes in Milan, we arrived in Zurich after dark. Snow covered the ground, and white Christmas lights twinkled in the trees. The next morning our Beirut friends, Ivan and Virginia Lathrop, drove us to the European Nazarene Bible College. A week later we flew to California to spend Christmas with our family.

Through God's grace, we had survived living under the shadow of war, in the shadow of His wings.

God Is Unfailing

THE FAITH OF A CHILD

C. M. Freeman

*W*alking out of church, I was stunned. The pastor had announced that Tom, an elder, was removed from the elder board and had left the church. He had left his family for another woman.

How could this be? I knew his sweet wife, Lydia, and their son, James, a young man with Down syndrome. I'll never forget how on that wintry cold day, sun bright in a blinding sort of way, I felt a chill deeper than winter's frosty bite.

Lydia faithfully continued attending church with James. They were at many of the events at church: morning and evening services, church dinners, prayer meetings, and Bible classes. I prayed that God's loving arms would surround them during this storm. As I thought of Tom, I prayed he would return to his faith and his family. But weeks blurred into months, and each season passed into the next.

James was well loved in church. I couldn't help but notice him, not only because of his Down syndrome, but also because of his persistence in asking for prayer for his dad. Once I took a Bible class with James; he always arrived a little early and asked the teacher to pray for his dad. James consistently asked everyone in our large church—from the pastor to the men's group to our class—to pray for his dad to return home.

Missionaries will tell amazing stories of people receiving the Lord.

The animist in Africa is freed from fear of the spirit world when he learns of God's love. The atheist in a communist country learns there is a creator and joyfully accepts a personal relationship with the living Lord. Missionaries thrill me with these accounts.

But what about fellow believers who fall into sin? Where is God's power there?

Lydia said right from the start that she would take Tom back and forgive him. Her lack of bitterness and willingness to forgive reflected the heart of Christ. Yet, a couple of years passed, and Tom's situation seemed the same. He would visit and see James on the weekends, but he wouldn't repent.

> He always arrived a little early
> and asked the teacher to pray for his dad.

Every year on Mother's Day our church gives flowers to honor various mothers in the church—ones with the most children, the newest mother, the oldest mother, etc. Yet this year, for the first time, our pastor wanted to honor women with different circumstances. Knowing of Lydia's trials, he called James to the platform to give flowers to his mother. Before a crowd of a thousand or so, James walked up to receive the flowers, but then he reached for the microphone. James thanked the pastor for the flowers and asked him to pray for his dad. Something gripped me. Aside from my tears and being moved at James's dedication, I had a renewed sense of urgency to pray for Tom.

Several weeks later I was driving home from work, when I sensed God prompting me to urgently pray for Tom. I prayed that Jesus would protect Tom from Satan and that Tom's faith would be restored. I prayed that he would come back to Jesus and his family. Thinking of

James, I earnestly asked God to answer my prayers. I wanted James to see the answer to his prayers so that God would have the victory—not Satan. I prayed several times that week with the sense that Tom was in spiritual danger. I wanted to tell Lydia about those prayers, but busyness and a summer schedule kept me from it.

Two months later, toward the end of the summer, while I was walking on the beach, I saw a woman who also went to my church. She asked if I had heard about James. My heart flip-flopped. She told me that James was seriously ill in the hospital. I prayed for him, in fear that he wouldn't live to see the answer to his prayers for his dad.

A few weeks later I saw Lydia and asked how James was doing. Thankfully he was much better. Then I asked if she had heard from Tom. Her eyes sparkled as she said they were going for counseling together. Tom had told her that he knew he needed to repent, and he had felt like Satan was chasing him. My breath stopped. I hadn't gotten to tell her about my prayers yet, so I asked her the timing of this. Lydia said it was shortly after the Mother's Day service.

God is ever on His redemptive mission to free people from sin, and He had a plan for this fractured family! I'm amazed that God prompted me to pray at the time when Tom started to realize he needed to change his life. The God who sees everything helped me notice James's persistence, and God delighted in James's faithfulness and trust.

Several years have passed. Today I walked into the fellowship hall at church. Threading my way through the crowd of faces, I saw Tom and James together. I walked over to them, welcomed Tom back, and rejoiced at God's answer to prayer. Tom thanked me for my prayers, but I said it was all because of James. Seeing James's persistence sparked my prayers.

God Is Unfailing

Looking at James, I said, "He sees things more clearly."

James's heart is fully committed to God. With a simple and pure love, he persisted after God and prayed for what God would want—his mom and dad together again. James knew what was broken and knew who could fix it.

> James knew what was broken and knew who could fix it.

Today James sat proudly next to his parents at the worship service. With a beaming smile, he sat with his arm around his father, who was gratefully reunited with his heavenly Father.

God Is Mighty

A "GOD-INCIDENCE"

David Michael Smith

*I*t was a Saturday night in October near Baltimore, Maryland. My wife, Geralynn, and I were sitting in our car, which was idling at a traffic light on Honeygo Boulevard, a busy highway near the suburb of Parkville and the popular, always congested White Marsh Mall. Honeygo is a major artery that leads into one of America's longest and most journeyed interstates, I-95, which runs from northern Maine to southern Florida. That ten-lane expressway was our planned destination.

We had visited my father-in-law that afternoon and were on our way back home to southern Delaware, a two-hour trek. We were both tired and wanted to be home. All we wanted was a safe, fast ride, and then an eight-hour appointment with our pillows—nothing more.

The roads were heaving with motorists. Both left-turn lanes were full, and we sat in the right-hand line of steel and wheels. Everyone appeared to be heading either toward the mall or from it, with steady traffic pouring into and from the nearby interstate. I impatiently shifted into neutral, a long-standing habit of mine while sitting at stop lights. I fiddled with the radio, another habit of impatience.

The light turned green, and the cars in front of our vehicle lunged forward, as if at a drag raceway. I grabbed the shifter, which was located in the center console between two bucket seats, and pulled it toward the D for drive.

But something was awry.

The knob held no tension, and I couldn't get the car into gear. It was clearly broken and moved as if unconnected to anything. My wife looked at my pale face.

"What's wrong?" she asked.

"I don't know," I flatly replied. "I can't get the car into gear."

Behind us car horns began to blare, but I ignored them, too scared and too focused on the situation. If I had a list of places *not* to break down, this would have been at the top of the list.

"Try again," Geralynn urged.

> If I had a list of places *not* to break down, this would have been at the top of the list.

"Look," I replied, staring at the gear shifter, "something's wrong. Maybe the transmission dropped."

I had always heard that was a huge bill. I felt like crawling under a rock.

Other cars began to navigate around us, sometimes dangerously pulling out into the main lanes of traffic. I tried the shifter again and again. I turned the car off and then restarted it, hoping it might somehow reset itself. Nothing worked, and I was beginning to panic. We felt helpless, stranded in the intersection of a busy roadway, on a hectic weekend night, in the suburbs of a major metropolitan area, encased in darkness. I hastily and mutely prayed for God to send help.

The light again turned red, and a new line of vehicles gathered around our disabled car. I turned on my hazard lights, and despite the flashing cries for help, no one stopped to offer any. We cracked our windows and heard insults and curses from passing motorists. It was as if many of our highway brethren thought we planned our misfortune to disrupt their commute. I wanted to fast forward my life and put this frightening episode in the past tense!

Suddenly on the passenger side of the car we saw a pulsating, swirling hue of red and then heard a single siren blast. It was a patrolman in a county cruiser. We were saved!

"Thank you, Lord," I breathed, feeling dumb for letting my fears get the best of me. This uniformed savior would radio for a tow truck, guard us from inattentive motorists, and keep watch with us. I laughed with a sigh of relief.

Without exiting his unit, the policeman rolled down his window and called over to us, asking if we were okay. His attention quickly turned from us as his radio crackled to life. A few seconds later, he turned back to us, his expression grim.

"Sorry folks, but I need to leave you here for a bit. Got an emergency call, something bad. I'll have someone drop by and give you a hand. Meantime, keep your emergency flashers on, and be careful." And then he left with squealing tires, a look of concern painted across his stern face. My fears returned, amplified.

We sat there in silence for minutes, but it felt much longer. More belligerent drivers zoomed by, laughing at our misfortune, yelling obscenities. I peered into my mirrors and around us for any signs of law enforcement. Nothing.

Then the unlikeliest of drivers pulled over and stopped next to us.

"You guys alright?" he slurred. He was young and obviously drunk. Still, I thought, he was the only person to check on us in the fifteen minutes or more since our nightmare had started.

"Broken down," I said stoically, "something with the transmission."

"You know anybody to call?"

God Is Mighty

Geralynn's father could help us, certainly, but we needed to locate a phone since we didn't have a cell phone.

"Yes," I replied, "can you give me a lift to a service station?" In the distance, perhaps a mile away, was an Exxon station, its large, illuminated red-white-and-blue sign signaling an oasis of safety.

The guy, who said his name was Mike, took me to the station where I placed my call, then returned me to my wife.

After Mike left, my father-in-law showed up, followed by a AAA truck, and our car was eventually towed. We borrowed my mother-in-law's car to finally drive home, hours after our original departure time, exhausted, frustrated, yet strangely feeling blessed.

> The events of the previous night replayed in my mind, in slow motion, like the pieces of a mysterious puzzle falling into place.

The next day, after a lengthy night's rest, we learned from the garage that the problem was not our transmission or anything close to it. Apparently a simple, ordinary spring, total value equaling two dollars, had become disconnected. The car was repaired, and I was ecstatic.

Then the phone rang again with a piercing shrill.

"Did you guys hear about that accident last night?" my father-in-law asked.

"No, what accident?" I asked.

"Out on I-95, horrible crash, four deaths, several others injured. It's in the paper this morning and all over the TV."

"When did that happen?"

"Oh, right around nine p.m. the paper said."

Suddenly the events of the previous night replayed in my mind, in slow motion, like the pieces of a mysterious puzzle falling into place.

A "God-incidence"

The officer being called away from our predicament . . . the time our car broke down . . . the simple yet strange circumstances surrounding our breakdown . . . the ashy flares we saw later en route to home along the interstate's shoulder. A quick mental calculation put our car smack dab or very close to the fiery crash scene. Yet we avoided the possible tragedy, thanks in part to a broken shifter spring, a shifter that had been used thousands of times but, for some unknown reason, only slipped loose on that fateful evening.

Was this the hand of God, or merely a coincidence? Or as some people call it, a "God-incidence" where we later saw his fingerprints.

I know one thing: a personal experience that felt miserably stressful turned out to be just fine. The event that we thought was a curse was really a bounteous blessing.

God Is Mighty

God Is Compassionate

GOING TO SEMINARY ON DRUG MONEY

Sandra Glahn

*C*all me Sandra—daughter of Ann, daughter of Velma, daughter of Ella . . . going all the way back to Eve. Like the dinosaur, now extinct, I'm a Sandra-saur. I will never give birth. The genetic line stops with me.

I grew up in what might be most accurately described as "a loud family." Think of the German version of *My Big Fat Greek Wedding*, and you'll have a pretty good picture of our family. The fourth of five children, I used to eat pizza cold out of the fridge because if I heated it up, someone would catch a whiff and make me share.

My brothers loved art and music. My sisters loved to sew. I was the one who loved babies. I earned most of my spending money taking care of neighbor kids and helping one of the moms do physical therapy with her disabled twins. I sensed I was destined for motherhood. Never once did I ever imagine that I might someday face infertility.

The home my parents created was always bustling with activity and noise. If someone came to our house after school, he or she would hear one of us practicing piano scales, another playing tuba, and a little screeching on a violin and a viola. When we had friends over, we'd play Pit and Twister—not the quietest options. Television was out. We had an old black-and-white version nobody wanted to bother with. And if we got bored, we could always pound the drum and crash the cymbals.

Despite the relative insanity, except when I had to wait in line for a bathroom, I loved living in a large family. I never felt lonely. I always had a cheering section for viola concerts. And the seven-part harmony on cross-country road trips gave me glimpses of heaven.

When I went to college, I had no career plans. I wanted to learn, but I mostly envisioned myself married to Gary, my high school sweetheart, and having a large family. After my second and his third year of schooling, we married. And once we earned our bachelor's degrees, we moved to Dallas so Gary could earn a master's in theology. Five years after we tied the knot, we figured it was high time to expand our family of two. We decided that, if God willed, we'd have three kids.

But a year went by with no success.

And then another.

I went to the doctor.

A third year passed.

And then it happened—the positive pregnancy test!

Whooping and cheering, we called our families. Everyone rejoiced with words like "finally!" and "hurrah!" and "yahoo!" But joy turned to tragedy a few days later when I miscarried.

> Joy turned to tragedy a few days later
> when I miscarried.

And then it happened again. And again.

It happened a total of seven times. Finally, after a decade of hope and despair, doctors determined that I had an immune-system disorder. My body was attacking the embryo as it would a disease. Reeling from the shock, we took a year off from treatment.

After that, we pursued adoption. In three years' time, we were matched with three birth mothers, and all three changed their minds

God Is Compassionate

at the last minute. In one case I'd even gone through birthing classes with the girl.

The spiritual crisis hit harder than the emotional one. What did God want me to do with my life? The wound struck at the core of my womanhood and my limited view of what I was made to do. What did he want me to do and be?

Wasn't giving birth the epitome of womanhood? I'd always heard that a woman's highest calling was motherhood. Where did I fit into that ideal?

> The wound struck at the core of my womanhood and my limited view of what I was made to do.

As I looked around and prayed about what I should do with my life, I considered that I had a degree in Bible. I had taught a women's Bible study at my church, and I found joy in the process. Should I go to seminary? Before long, both my husband and my pastor's wife urged me to do exactly that.

But graduate school is expensive, and medical bills had drained our finances. I had nearly decided against going for that reason when a woman called to tell me she would cover my tuition. With trembling hands, I completed the application, and within a few weeks I received my acceptance letter for the spring semester. Classes started in January.

We spent the Christmas holidays visiting my sister on the West Coast, and while we were there, I received a call from this woman. She let me know that she couldn't pay for my tuition after all. I hung up the phone and cried.

Lord, if I can't be a mom and I can't be a student, what am I supposed to do with my life?

We returned home from that trip on a Sunday night, and the Monday tuition deadline loomed over me. We didn't have the $1,950 that I needed within twenty-four hours.

The following afternoon when the mail arrived, I went to the box, and the surprise that met me was one of the most meaningful "God sightings" of my life. I opened an envelope from my doctor's office and found an unexpected check for $1,900. As it turned out, because he was both a physician and a licensed pharmacist, my doctor was able to legally give my unused medications to another patient, who graciously wrote a check and had him send it to me.

My husband joked that I may be the only student to attend seminary using "drug money."

Today we have a daughter who joined our family thirteen years ago through the miracle of adoption, and I teach at the same seminary where I began that spring as a student. In the years that followed the surprise in my mailbox, I've found my purpose: I was born to teach. And I have hundreds of "children" living all over the world.

God Is Compassionate

God Is Wonderful

A Down Payment, and More

Lynne Gentry

$\mathcal{I}$knew I was marrying a preacher. What I didn't know was how much a life of ministry would cost me.

The day we got back from our honeymoon, my starry-eyed husband convinced me he needed graduate-school training to be properly equipped to save the world.

Anxious to prove I could be the sacrificial preacher's wife, I agreed. I helped him cram our wedding gifts into the trunk of his souped-up Chevy Nova, and we were off. As we barreled toward his grad school, I stuffed my concerns as to how we were going to pay for this extra education. Instead of counting the cost, I focused on the perfect picture I'd painted in my mind: our serving side by side happily ever after. God had been faithful to provide a husband, and I expected God to faithfully provide our livelihood.

Within a couple of days we found a cheap apartment and I found a job at a law firm. The apartment was small and the cockroaches were big, but we were in love, and God was on our side. For the next three years my husband threw himself into his graduate studies while I rode a bus to work. Although things were tight, we made friends with other grad-school couples over bowls of macaroni and cheese and late-night board games. Living on love and school loans, I told myself not to worry: God had everything under control. Hadn't He provided my job to pay the rent and the loan money to pay the tuition? Surely we could count on Him to continue his faithfulness.

Three years later my husband was set to graduate. Proud and excited, I tried not to think about how his becoming highly educated had put us deeply in debt. I told myself God was up for any financial test and would provide.

So we had a baby. Even though our blessed bundle arrived three weeks before my husband's last finals and two months before he had a job, I tried not to worry as the rent came due. Sitting cross-legged on the floor, a newborn cradled in my lap, I carefully rolled the change in the big glass jar we kept on the dresser: $57.32. Not enough for rent, but enough for the five-hundred-mile drive to his first job interview— if we ate peanut butter sandwiches and didn't stop to spend the night in a hotel.

I buried my fears under the last package of diapers from the baby shower our friends had given us, slammed the trunk on the Nova, and prayed God would remain faithful. Neither of us brought up the question of how we could buy gas for the trip back if the church didn't call us. Fortunately, we didn't have to worry because the small church hired us on the spot. They even gave us an advance on our first paycheck. God had provided again.

For the next eight years we lived in the church's parsonage, not owning our own home or building any equity. As our family grew, so did the interest on the grad-school loans we struggled to pay off. At the end of the month, we didn't have an extra nickel to stash away for a single rainy day, let alone for the impossible dream of one day buying our own house. I told myself that missionaries in Africa didn't own houses, and I knew God loved them; so I had no choice but to believe that God loved me and that He would be faithful.

But the real test came when we had an opportunity to move. This

God Is Wonderful

new church was bigger and in a larger city, but they did not own a parsonage. The preacher was expected to buy his own house.

The church flew us to town to spend a week searching for a house and hooked us up with a wonderful Realtor. She asked what we wanted in a home. Too embarrassed to say "No down payment," I told her that schools and neighborhood were important and that we had to keep our options within a reasonable price range. We spent the next few days going from house to house, each more beautiful than the last. Each in our price range—if only we had the required down payment.

> The apartment was small and the cockroaches were big, but we were in love, and God was on our side.

That night, my husband and I returned to our hotel room, exhausted and disappointed. We could not buy a house. We couldn't even buy the Realtor lunch. Out loud, I said a house did not matter. But on the inside, I railed at a God who would saddle us with so much debt and so many years of so little pay that we could not put a roof over our children's heads. Didn't He know all that we had sacrificed for Him?

Then I tried something that had never occurred to me before concerning God's provision: I prayed.

In the past, I just assumed God would do the right thing and provide. After all, weren't we doing our share by giving up our lives to serve Him? The least He could do was provide. And He always had. Textbook money here. Food money there. Even gas money for that first interview trip.

But this time the stakes were higher. This was a home for my kids. So, far into the night I begged God to make it possible for us to buy a house.

In the morning we had one last meeting with the Realtor before we were to leave for the airport. We decided to tell her that we would just rent until we could find something that suited us . . . something without a down payment. I told myself that was God's provision, His way of keeping us from sinking further into debt.

The Realtor knocked on our hotel door. When we opened the door, we were surprised to see her standing there with a grin on her face and a signed check in her hand . . . our down payment. Even more surprising, the check also covered the exact amount of the total student loan we'd spent the last ten years paying off, plus an added $5,000 for the interest. God had provided in a most unexpected way by having the church give us a signing bonus as a welcome gift. This had never happened before in that church and has never happened again in that church.

Twenty years later, sitting in my comfortable kitchen, I marvel at the mysterious workings of God. The way our loving heavenly Father provides when I trust and the way He provides when I don't.

Thankfully, God's faithfulness does not depend upon mine.

If I had it to do all over again, would I marry a preacher? Only if God agrees to squeeze into the front seat of our old Chevy.

God Is Wonderful

God Is Defender

GOD NEVER TAKES A VACATION

Linda Jett

"*J*im, this day looks like an advertisement for the perfect vacation."

I marveled at the view. The sun sparkled across East Lake on a clear, crisp September Thursday. With schools back in session, only a few fishing boats dotted the 1,050-acre expanse of this remote volcanic lake.

My husband and I settled into our kayaks to explore the obsidian-studded shoreline at a leisurely pace. Our challenge for the day was ahead: a five-mile paddle around the lake's perimeter.

Why don't we schedule vacations more often? I mused. The splash of fish and the call of birds marked nature's peaceful rhythms. My body welcomed this change of pace.

After several hours of paddling, however, we encountered a phenomenon the kayaking guidebooks had noted. An afternoon wind pushed the water into waves, slicing our peace into shreds.

"Let's aim for that landing," Jim shouted over the walkie-talkie we used to communicate in our separate kayaks. He pointed at a gentle slope near a campground boat dock, the first we'd seen since we set out.

An hour later, we lowered our sore bodies onto soft, dry towels on the lake's shore. We ate a snack and commented about how quickly the lake's mood had changed. "Think we can make it back to our original launch point?" we asked each other. Middle-aged novices at this sport, we questioned our limits.

As we rested, we watched two elderly fishermen struggle to load their fishing boat onto a boat trailer. Every time they lined the boat up with the partially submerged trailer, the wind snatched it away before they could pull the prow forward.

"Think they need help?" I queried.

"Yep." Jim hoisted his strong, heavy frame and sauntered over. "Could you use a hand?"

"Sure," they agreed. Jim waded waist-deep into the water between the dock and the boat trailer to steer and guide the prow of the boat. One man moved to the far end of the dock to steady the stern. The other climbed into the bed of the pickup to guide the boat's rope into the winch.

Suddenly, the driverless pickup popped out of gear and rolled into the water. With the partially submerged pickup blocking my view, my precious husband disappeared somewhere in the water on the other side.

"God, help!" I prayed aloud. "We need your angels now!"

I jumped up, grabbed our towels, and rushed toward the dock where I had last seen my husband.

By the time I got there, Jim was standing waist-deep in the water. Ice-cold water dripped from his head as he climbed onto the dock. I looked down. His right removable pant leg hung, partially unsnapped from the shorts. Blood began to show along the edges of a long, white gash in his leg.

"You're hurt!" I exclaimed.

He looked down, surprised by the blood. "I guess the cold water numbed my legs."

Jim's Boy Scout training took over. He remained the ultimate problem solver, even in a crisis! Determined to finish the task, he

God Is Defender

calmly secured the fishermen's boat to the now-submerged trailer.

The commotion drew several older campers from their sites near the lake. One experienced outdoorsman backed his truck to the water line and he attached a chain to the bumper of the sunken truck. As the truck on land strained forward, water poured out through the windows and door frames of the waterlogged pickup. Slowly it emerged, like a monster from the deep. The boat and trailer followed behind.

Mission accomplished, Jim climbed the hill to a bench. He sank down, examined his wound, and then wrapped it with his wet handkerchief. He methodically reattached his pant leg and propped up the injured leg. "Looks like I won't be finishing this trip in the kayak."

"We need to get you to a hospital, don't we?" I reviewed our options. "There's no cell phone coverage up here. Our car's parked several miles away in another campground. I don't know this lake. Do you think I can find the car? Should I try kayaking there alone?"

"No," Jim declared. "You need to find a ride back to the car. That's the safest way."

"Can I help?" One of the older campers asked as he ambled over.

"Uh, yes. I need a ride back to our car," I answered. But internally I processed, *Don't panic. Don't give any of these older people a reason for a heart attack.* I slid into the pickup's passenger seat, but intent on finding the right campground, I barely listened to my good Samaritan's comments as his truck rattled along the unfamiliar road.

"There it is." My finger shook as I pointed toward a parking spot near the lake.

Had God prompted Jim to choose a parking spot that was clearly visible from the main road?

At last in our own car, I prayed aloud as I drove back toward the place where I had left my husband. *God, usually Jim takes care of me. I have a tendency to get lost. Help me drive safely. Go before me. Guide me.*

Lord, please protect Jim from hyperthermia or shock or too much blood loss. Help me stay focused and calm. Help us find a hospital. Grant me your peace in the midst of this circumstance.

I pulled up to find Jim still wrapped in a towel. With his right leg propped up, he looked like a tourist taking a leisurely rest break. Below, however, the wind whipped the waves into whitecaps onto the shore.

"Let's load the kayaks," Jim directed. He hobbled to the boats. Together we loaded the kayaks on top of the car and tied them down. Relieved to have finished the job, he slid into the passenger seat with a sigh.

My leg was pinned and I was pulled under. I couldn't keep my head above water.

Jim recounted the details as I carefully wound our vehicle down the mountainside, curve after torturous curve. "All of a sudden the pickup was coming at me. There was no time to react. The trailer jackknifed. It trapped me between the trailer hitch and the pickup. My leg was pinned and I was pulled under. I couldn't keep my head above water. I prayed, wondering if this was how God intended for my life on earth to end. Then, suddenly, I felt the boat trailer lift. I was free. I still don't know how it happened. I can't explain it."

We glanced at each other. We both knew. It had to be God! Neither of the elderly fishermen had the physical strength to move the sunken boat trailer. It's likely they hadn't even seen Jim go under.

"I'm glad it was me," Jim reflected. "I don't think either of them could have survived being pinned under water like that." He shifted his leg to find a more comfortable position.

After an hour and a half and a maze of blue H signs, we arrived at

God Is Defender

St. Charles Medical Center in Bend, Oregon. I dropped Jim off at the ER door. When I returned from the crowded parking lot, the nurse directed me to a triage room. Two emergency cases, an older man with a heart attack and a logger with a broken back, took precedence, so Jim and I waited together.

"Miraculously, no bones were broken!" the ER doctor exclaimed after viewing Jim's X-ray several hours later. A compassionate nurse deadened Jim's right calf and knee, bit by bit with a needle, as I cringed. She cleaned his fifteen-inch wound, sutured, and then bandaged it. When she finished, the ER doctor returned to the room with explicit instructions: "Your vacation is over. Fill the prescriptions. Go back home tomorrow and check in with your family doctor."

Two brightly colored kayaks announced our car's position in a far lot as we emerged from the hospital. We dutifully filled the prescriptions and then ate. Quietly, we inched our way through miles of stop-and-go construction in the dark before the lights of our motel appeared, a welcome sight.

We missed the last two lakes we'd hoped to kayak, but we survived our vacation. Reality replaced shock. I might have left that lake as a widow. Even today, several years later, Jim's scar reminds us that God never takes a vacation, even when we do!

God Is Light

MESSENGERS OF LIGHT

Gary L. Crawford

"Slow it down! Slow it down!" All of us in the back of a two-ton army truck yelled at the young driver careening down the curvy road into Monterey, California. Hanging on to the bench seats, we banged into one another, first one way then the other. Some of the guys cursed the kid in the driver's seat.

A guy near the front of our bench seats banged on the window and screamed at the driver. "For crying out loud, we can't even hang on back here. Slow the rig down."

Then it happened. A fifteen-second, life-changing rollover. I remember crying out, "God, if you'll let me live, I'll quit smoking." I made a greater bargain with God, too: I promised to serve Him.

It sounds trite to say, "My life flashed before me." Yet it did. Most of my life I'd attended church twice on Sunday and prayer meetings on Wednesday, and had been the all-around good guy. As a teen I'd dedicated my life to the Lord, then met a young lady, asked her to marry me in a few years, graduated from high school, and signed up for the army reserves.

Away from Mom, the church influence, and my girl, I did what a lot of soldiers did—experimented with gambling, drinking, and smoking.

In those few seconds on the mountain, as I was slammed from one soldier to another, I knew my heart wasn't right with God. I prayed like I hadn't prayed in months, "Lord, save us all."

After the truck suddenly tipped and rolled once, it stopped against a lone tree halfway down the mountain. The truck's tarp and hoops covered us as we lay in a pile. Guys groaned. Some, seriously hurt, screamed in pain and fear. Others cried. I ended up at the bottom of the pack.

Later that day, when the ambulances drove us into the medical unit, I knew God had spared my life for a far greater purpose than just living.

> Away from Mom, the church influence,
> and my girl, I did what a lot of soldiers did.

I'd like to say I kept every promise made on the hillside, but I didn't. I finished my army stint and went home to marry Kathy, the girl of my dreams. Soon after, I started work in a mill to support us. There I met Ben.

Ben was one of those nice people who show up in most places. He worked with the maintenance crew, and because he checked the oil levels on the different machines around me, I saw him often. He was old enough to be my granddad, a homely sort of guy who always wore bib overalls.

I soon noticed he seemed different from the other guys. Ben always had a smile on his face and a positive attitude. Before long I realized Ben didn't swear or tell disgusting jokes.

Once in a while I'd lapse into one of those bad habits I'd told the Lord I'd quit, but Ben never did preach at me.

One day during my break time I headed to a rooftop for a smoke. When I climbed the ladder, I saw Ben kneeling in prayer. That was just one of many times I happened upon Ben talking to God. Over the years, I felt the Lord led me to those lonely spots as a reminder of where my life should be spent. Even after Ben retired, the picture of him kneeling during the day stayed in my mind.

A few years later, our mill went on strike. The younger generation wanted a new union; the oldsters—those who'd worked there twenty years or more—were against the strike. George Rogers, a man I met the first day I entered the local church, stood steadfast against the strike but took time off along with the younger workers.

"Don't believe in crossing a picket line," George said. "We need to stick together." Then he changed the subject. "The church board voted to upgrade the parking lot. Anyone who's not crossing the picket line want to join me here tomorrow and work on the parking lot?"

The next morning it rained a good Washington gully washer. I figured I might as well sling rock and help upgrade the parking lot rather than sit around.

George and I were the only ones heaving gravel in the downpour that day. When Kathy showed up with lunch, George told us about how God saved his life during World War II.

At thirty-two he'd enlisted in the navy as a pharmacist second class. Often he was called upon to tend the wounded. One day while he was on the ship's deck, a doctor sent him below for medical supplies. Before George returned to the deck, a bomber hit the ship. Every man in George's medical unit was killed, except him.

"I'd been raised in the church and served the Lord in my younger years," George said. "But like many in the navy, I wasn't serving God with my whole heart. That day, when the plane bombed our unit, I knew the Lord had spared my life. Yet for some reason, I felt reluctant to truly sell out to God that day."

George's story sounded like my rollover on the mountain.

George was moved to another ship where one morning he was

standing on the deck. "I saw a Japanese kamikaze plane headed straight for us. I dropped to my knees and said, 'God, if you save my life, I'll serve you the rest of my life.' That bomber veered away from our ship and crashed into the sea. I made my peace with God that day."

George promised to pray for me, and I knew he did. Still it seemed like the cares of everyday life got between me and my goals to seek God. I waffled between wanting to serve the Lord and really doing it.

Seven years after slinging that gravel, I finally stood in church and said, "I've completely sold out to God. When our house sells, I'll move my family to Colorado Springs to attend Bible college."

George wept.

Attending Bible college wasn't easy to do with a family. Kathy worked, and I attended school. Our meager income didn't cover all the school expenses. When I arrived at school, another student said, "Where's your textbook?"

"Don't have the money just yet. I'll take good notes," I told him.

I didn't even know the classmate well, but I'll never forget his concern. I saw his eyes fill with tears. The next night after I'd settled into my seat, that student, a guy without a lot of money, dropped a book on my desk. "You need this."

That gift did more than help me study; it taught me to share with others when the Lord supplies our needs.

I thank God for these men, these messengers of light who led me back to Him. And He continues to direct me on the right path as I allow Him to lead me.

God Is Salvation

WHO HUNG THE MOON (UPSIDE DOWN)?

Julie Arduini

"*W*hat did you just say? You're pregnant?"

The bearded volunteer fireman let out a low whistle and retreated from the 1998 Voyager carnage. I remained strapped in the seat, upside down, mystery drips falling into the ditch where the van rested. The drops to my right were scarlet, but I knew it wasn't blood, at least not my blood. Was it brake fluid? Dye from the sweater in the front seat? The firemen shouted commands and made guesses.

"How far along? Do you feel any pain?"

As the bearded one poked his head in the driver window, glass scattered below my head.

"Ten weeks. I was actually on the way to the hospital for blood work. I'm high risk because of infertility."

I listened to my voice, shocked at the confidence and coherence of my words. My hands shook. All this time to conceive a child, and in one swift move I had fast-forwarded a Kim Boyce tape to hear "Who Hung the Moon?" and ended up looking upside down at the moon in a ditch!

"Well ma'am, we'll get you to the hospital. What's your dog's name?"

I tried to turn to see our dog-shelter treasure, Casey, who went everywhere with me, but the seat belt was so tight that I couldn't turn.

"Casey. Is he okay?"

"Appears to be very protective of you. One of your neighbors agreed to take the dog while we get you to the hospital. He's getting gloves just in case the dog gets overprotective and tries to attack him."

I instinctively reached for the seat-belt release so I could pet my dog. I couldn't touch my baby yet, but at least I could touch Casey.

"Ma'am, don't push that. Your neck could be . . . "

Too late. I clicked the button and landed on the van roof. Casey leaped to me, ignoring the sea of glass.

"I'm okay, I know it. The baby . . . I just need to hear the baby is okay."

> "I'm okay, I know it.
> The baby . . . I just need to hear the baby is okay."

I heard another fire truck's slow blare in the distance.

A year ago, my husband, Tom, and I had made the outskirts of Beaver Dams, New York, our home. Every time we'd heard the siren from one of the old fire trucks, we'd giggled. This one had to be a circa 1940 truck. And this was the vessel God would use for my rescue?

I reassured Casey as the men planned my escape. I could hear their heavy boots stomp as they circled the van.

"Hey, great news, it's just brake fluid. You turned off the ignition when you landed; a smart choice."

Unlike my overcorrective driving, which caused the accident to begin with.

"My husband. Someone needs to call him. Please tell him I'm okay."

I tried to shout above the siren, but only Casey looked at me. I determined to let myself out of the van and get to a phone myself. The bearded man stuck his head in the window again. Casey growled.

"I'm terrible with names. What is it again?"

"Julie."

"Julie, we can't have you move around. You need to keep still until we get you on the backboard and out of here. It's standard procedure."

I recognized a new liquid. This time tears slid down my cold face.

"My husband. Someone call him. Please let him know I'm okay."

"The sheriff just got here; I'm sure he'll get the number and call for you. You're one lucky lady; your neighbor by the ditch had the day off and heard you crash. He was on the scene in less than two minutes. He's also ready to take the dog."

"Casey."

The bearded volunteer nodded. "Right, Casey. Dogs by nature are defensive when they sense their owner is in danger. He seems friendly, but we don't want to take any chances with you, your baby, or us."

This time I nodded, still stroking his wet fur. I whimpered good-bye, as a pair of gloved hands slid through the passenger window and reached for Casey.

"Good doggie. That's it, Casey. We're going to help her. We promise."

I couldn't keep track of the men. All were wearing yellow coats and the same kind of thick waterproof boots.

"Hello, Julie, is it?"

I turned to the driver window again, mad at myself for moving so much when I'd been instructed not to.

"That's me, just hanging around."

The sheriff smiled and introduced himself.

"The paramedics are here with the backboard, and the tow truck is almost here. Your van will most likely end up about ten miles away in Watkins Glen. Has anyone told you how lucky you are? I've never seen anything like it."

I tried to steady my hand to keep focused.

"I don't believe in luck. I believe in God."

"Well, God did something amazing with this accident. Besides the glass, you're sitting on your tapes and your Bible."

"Right, I had them in the back seat. I'm sure they flew forward in the accident."

"True enough. But the miraculous part is you had two bowling balls in the back. Pure gravity would have those balls flying to the front at you. Yet, one of the guys found them out the back. Like I said, never saw anything like it."

Until I heard a doctor tell me the baby was fine, I had to let everyone else find the miracles. I couldn't comprehend the devastation of the accident until I was away from it.

"Okay, time to get you out and to the hospital. Everything will be just fine."

The sheriff tipped his hat and started to leave, but I called out for him to wait.

"Can you call my husband? He was going to meet me. He'll be worried."

"I'll make sure he knows you're okay."

I took a breath, trying to get a hold of the tears.

"Make sure he knows the baby is okay?"

The sheriff noted my apprehension. "So far looks like the bad news is about the van. Looks like it was brand-new."

The tears poured down my cheeks as I nodded, the sheriff out of sight. The firemen were working on the door panel, requesting that I stop moving. Even my shoulders wobbled; I couldn't stop. I felt fine, had no signs of miscarriage. The sheriff called the scene a miracle, yet I had to know the baby was fine.

The paramedic who wheeled me into my temporary ER accommodations set the brake on the gurney. "Unfortunately for you, we had a multicar accident come in before you. The doctors are with those patients and will get to you as soon as they can." All I could see was sterile ceiling.

"Can you let me out of all this? I want to see what's going on."

The paramedic peered above me, his cheeks crimson from the cold.

"Sorry, especially with the pregnancy, we want you to move as little as possible. Hopefully the doctors will be right in. Your vitals were great in the ambulance. You should have seen the ride the bowling balls took out your back window. Craziest thing! Hey, take care now."

Footsteps faded, and I was left with nothing but the ceiling and medical sounds. Each machine beep, doctor page, and opening of ER doors gave way to increased panic. The isolation brought back the accident sounds. I wanted to touch my stomach but I had no reach. If I cried, there was no way to capture my tears. I was left with one option: prayer.

I thanked God for the quick neighborly response. I praised Him that Casey was okay. I lifted thanks for what the entire rural community seemed to be talking about regarding the accident—the bowling-ball miracle. Then I begged and pleaded that the baby would be declared healthy.

My one-on-one time with the Lord lasted longer than my examination. The ER doctor ordered tests, examined me thoroughly, and announced that people with paper cuts were in worse shape than I was. My husband and sister-in-law ran through the ER doors, and I finally felt it was okay to start talking miracles.

We drove by the scene, the van towed away. I saw two bowling balls shine outside the parameters of the ditch. God not only hung the moon, He manipulated gravity to spare our lives.

God Is Salvation

God Is Trustworthy

A Father's Unforgettable Day

David Michael Smith

I sat in a quiet, spotless hospital hallway dressed in island-blue scrubs, a floppy hairnet pinching my forehead, and matching booties covering my feet. I was very much alone in my thoughts. I anxiously waited for permission to enter the nearby operating room. I remember praying in short fragmented phrases. And I remember crying, my body frayed at the seams from tremors of quaking emotion.

"David? We're ready for you," the female nurse beckoned. I stood and followed her into the operating room, which was frigid cold and smelled of sanitizer. It was time. Finally.

I'd been waiting for this experience since I was sitting in eighth-grade French class talking to my best friend, Tim, in the back row.

"What do you want to do with your life when you get older?" he asked.

I replied without hesitation, "I want to be a dad."

Not the typical response for a boy of my age. He laughed and said I was crazy.

Fast forward to adulthood. When I married Geralynn, we shared a commitment to dream of raising a family. There was only one problem. Things would not go as we'd planned.

After nearly a decade of failed attempts to start a family, Geralynn and I were exhausted, frustrated, and outright depressed. We raised the white flag and gave up the fight, accepting our fate in life.

Along the way we tried fertility specialists, in vitro fertilization, artificial insemination, ovulation kits, and every imaginable nugget of wisdom from friends, neighbors, and coworkers. Except for two confirmed miscarriages, there wasn't a hint of success for us. Some couples simply were not intended to be parents, we thought.

Maybe we could live with this and it would be okay. But every time we considered the notion of never hearing the padding of small feet or the sound of childish giggling, or an excited, exuberant "Mommy" or "Daddy" on Christmas morning, a sour taste would rise up and ruin the day. So, after much prayer and consideration, we adopted. Our daughter was a beautiful pip-squeak of a girl from China with jet-black hair. Rebekah Joy was gorgeous, and we were happy.

Several months after the adoption, when we were fully settled in and our routines were in place, the bishop of our church announced in front of the entire congregation that he had received a word from God Almighty that Geri would give birth to a child. He added that the pregnancy would come soon and be healthy. We wept at the prospect of good news but were reluctant to buy into this, given our long track record.

"Whatever your will is, Lord," I prayed. "You're in charge here." It was a prayer I would later repeat often.

Shortly after that memorable Sunday morning, I was awakened at the crack of dawn as Geri pushed something in front of my foggy eyes. It first appeared to be an oversized, bulky thermometer. It was a pregnancy test stick. My wife was ecstatic.

There are two windows in the common home pregnancy test. I was well accustomed to reading the results, since we'd taken dozens over the years and never had one test positive. But this time, the lines in the test window were dark and strong. We were incredibly pregnant!

Soon afterward, we visited one of our many doctors to confirm the pregnancy and hear the baby's heartbeat. Hearing the rapid thumping

God Is Trustworthy

of our young child's heart through the tiny speaker took our breath away. The moment is permanently imprinted onto our souls.

The months to come were happy times, filled with ultrasounds (a boy was forecasted), celebrations, baby showers, and most important, a textbook healthy pregnancy from start to finish. The whole thing seemed easy, especially when we considered all the years of failed attempts. For us, it was God. He had to have orchestrated this.

"Uh, honey, I'm pretty sure my water just broke," Geri hesitantly said from the master bathroom one morning.

"You're kidding." I responded. It was 5:30 a.m., and we were getting ready for work. It was nearly three weeks before the baby's due date. And despite great preparation, planning, and scheduling, suddenly we felt utterly unready.

Nervously we made phone calls to family, packed bags, arranged for our daughter's care, and departed for the hospital.

After we checked into the hospital and received a room, we calculated that by the afternoon we'd be parents again. Geri was handling things remarkably well and looked like a runway model in her hospital gown. But minutes turned to hours, and the morning momentum stalled.

The doctor on duty prescribed a drug to induce labor, but this made no impact. He raised the dosage each hour until finally Geri was receiving the maximum amount. Then the contractions kicked into gear, becoming like the violent, crashing waves that announce a hurricane's arrival.

Dinner came and went, and the summer sun disappeared to the western side of the medical facility. We were tired, hungry, and anxious. Things were moving at a snail's pace.

Sometime after midnight, more than eighteen hours after Geri's water broke, the labor pains intensified, and at times it appeared Geri was in the throes of death rather than childbirth. I worried for her health and silently prayed for faster resolution and the birth of my son. A friendly nurse guaranteed that we'd have a new son by 2:00 a.m.

At 5:00 a.m., the baby was still very much in Geri's womb, refusing to budge. For the first time, the medical staff began talking in hushed tones about a Cesarean birth. They tried one more procedure that facilitated the usage of what appeared to be a small toilet plunger. Apparently our son's shoulders were entering the birth canal before the head, but no one knew exactly. All we knew was that birth should occur within twenty-four hours after the water breaks or the baby and mother face risks. We were concerned, even scared.

At approximately 7:00 a.m., we were taken down to the first floor where the operating room was located. I called my mother on a cell phone and broke down. We had been up all night and were exhausted, but we were really close to birth. Within the next hour, our son would be with us.

"May your will be done, Lord," I whispered as the nurse called me into the operating room.

I entered the OR to find Geri on her back, a hairnet on her head, and oddly happy. New medicine had numbed her entire abdominal region for the incisions into her uterus, and the contractions that haunted her through the night were gone. She joyfully couldn't feel a thing.

A large curtain seemed to sever Geri at the waist, so she and I didn't have to view the gruesome details of the surgery. However, I found myself fascinated and watched. I told Geri I loved her and was proud of her. We were ready; it was time.

Moments later the doctor reached into Geri's dissected midsection and, like a magician pulling the white rabbit out of a hat, extracted my son, Matthew Robert Smith, covered in hues of secretions, blood, and afterbirth.

God Is Trustworthy

I always thought this sight would be too horrid and ghastly to view firsthand, but it wasn't. In fact it was perhaps the most beautiful sight I've ever seen, on par with my bride on our wedding day and my daughter when we received her in China a year earlier.

I failed to successfully squeeze back the tide of tears that poured from my eyes. I wanted to grab him and just hold him to my chest. I thanked God and kissed Geri's forehead. I was finally a dad by birth.

After Matthew was cleaned and wrapped in a blue blanket, he was presented to Geri, who tenderly held him while she was stitched up. I trembled with excitement and love and touched his tiny fingers, which grabbed at mine. Words fail to describe our exhilaration.

And so our family of four was made complete on that June morning. It wasn't an easy journey. Many attributes contributed to our eventual success: faith, hope, and patience come to mind. But mostly our children are blessings from heavenly realms, gifts of grace, undeserved, but appreciated and accepted.

Dreams can come true when the Miracle Worker is involved. We know that firsthand.

God Is Righteous

THE CATCH OF THE DAY WAS NOT A FISH

Muriel Gladney

The art of fishing was part of Jesus' ministry. He even told the first disciples that he would teach them to be fishers of men.

God is still going fishing, but before He aimed His fishing rod in my direction, He first had to bait His hook with an extraordinary lure.

At the time, God was a myth as far as I was concerned. This perception started in my childhood and remained unwavering until just before my "Forty-and-over-the-hill" T-shirt was about to be replaced with one saying "Fifty and Nifty." On the other hand, William, the man God used as bait, had been raised in the knowledge of God.

William was a self-employed electrician. A mutual friend had given me his number for a potential job. Upon our meeting, I immediately sensed something different about him. Standing six foot two and built like a world-touring bodybuilder, his looks were almost secondary. What caught and held my attention was a sense of almost tangible inner peace in him that never wavered despite any chaotic situation.

The calmness that seemed to swirl around him drew me. Our relationship in turn grew. I often witnessed how the serenity of his inner strength drew people to him. More important, he came to love me beyond my human expectations.

God's bait was irresistible. I swallowed the bait—hook, line, and sinker.

During the following year, people often asked when William and I would get married. We initially thought it strange and ignored what we considered the ramblings of others. Approximately one and a half years after we met, yet again, a stranger walked up to us and asked if we were going to get married.

Later that evening, William asked, "Do you think we should get married?"

"I don't know, what do you think?" I answered.

Giggling like school kids, we started planning our wedding. Gazing into William's brown eyes, I knew I had met my soul mate.

Ten months after our wedding, our picture-perfect future shattered like a piece of dropped crystal.

William became unexpectedly ill on the way to one of our customary fishing trips. After an emergency trip to the hospital and several days of testing, William was diagnosed with terminal colon cancer. Surgery was ineffective. During his recuperation, William, who had never forced his faith on me, outwardly expressed his desire to return to his upbringing in the knowledge of God.

Much to my chagrin, William walked into the living room one Sunday morning and asked, "Can we go to church today?" William and I had never gone to church together, and his suggestion unnerved me.

My outward demeanor remained as calm as a waveless ocean. However, thoughts of his absurdity threatened to explode like volcanic lava. I felt threatened—even betrayed. In fact, I remember averting my eyes to hide the blaze of my fury. However, as though someone else were speaking for me, I heard what I later called my Judas lips saying, "Yes, dear."

As I stood in the bedroom laying out clothes for church, my actions baffled me.

However, God knew what was happening.

The Catch of the Day Was Not a Fish

Thereafter, we regularly attended services at church, where we were constantly besieged with mankind's platitudes and promises of spiritual healing. Overwhelmed with a spirit of helplessness, I watched as William shrunk to a skeletal replica of his former self.

His funeral took place on a Saturday. The next morning I awoke with an overpowering urge to attend services. Fighting against the irresistible pull, I stomped from room to room shouting at the empty walls about the futility of religion. I felt like a fish twisting and turning on a line. Unable to free myself, I dressed and drove to church.

I discovered later that God was tightening his line.

> I stomped from room to room shouting at the empty walls about the futility of religion.

During the drive, I could not help but see that spring was in the throes of rebirth, which only added insult to my grief. The rising sun displayed its beauty by spreading tendrils of ginger reds and carroty orange across the blue pallet of the heavens. The sky looked like a painter's masterpiece. As I exited my car in front of the church, the twittering of birds and their babies announced new beginnings. Conversely, the echoing click-click of my heels minus the thump-thump of William's heavy footsteps proclaimed death's victory.

As I started up the stairs to the church entrance, my feet froze on the third step. Before I could turn and flee, the doors burst open, I heard the congregation singing, and several smiling greeters declared, "Welcome, we love you in the Lord." I was like a fish caught in a net as a multitude of arms encircled me, pulling me into church.

God had me in the boat.

Week after week I returned and sat on the same pew where William and I had sat. The oak pew, however, offered only the coldness of dead

God Is Righteous

wood. William had forsaken his promise of forever and had abandoned me. I felt emotionally naked.

Seeking answers for myself seemed to be the only solution. I bought my first Bible, a concordance, and a lexicon in order to study what I had always considered to be the height of stupidity—the Bible.

Hooked and landed, a captive audience, God was about to start my training.

His Holy Spirit chose a Friday-evening Bible-study service to turn my upside-down life right side up.

The pastor was teaching on God's creation of Adam and Eve. Suddenly, he stepped out of the pulpit, brought a chair, and sat down directly in front of me. He later explained that the lost look on my face caused his reaction. He then reminded the congregation of when we made mud pies as children. He reached down and formed an imaginary figure before breathing into the make-believe form.

At that precise moment, the Holy Spirit entered my heart to reveal God's existence. It felt as though someone had shoved me back against the pew. Quicker than an eye could blink, I knew the truth of our creation by God. More importantly, I knew to whom I belonged.

However, God was not through with me yet. It was just the beginning.

God began to answer every question I presented to Him, confirming what I heard and saw through the Scriptures. I discovered that the Bible taught on marriage, fidelity, friendship, family, raising children, neighbors, and so on. The knowledge I thought I had gained from self-help books paled in comparison to God's truth and wisdom.

When God intervened in my life, His first act was to show me His creation. Then He revealed His everlasting love for me, and also for all of His creation.

Last but not least, He assured me that He would never toss me back out of the boat, no matter what I faced in life.

God Is Eternal

ARTIST, MEET THE MASTER

Sandi Banks

$\mathcal{W}$e all agreed that our Rocky Mountain summer had ended too quickly that year. Along with the autumn chill came the familiar, bittersweet process of bidding our summer students and staff farewell.

Every May to September, our ministry's humble campus came alive—the cabins, classrooms, dorms, porches, buses, and sports fields filled to overflowing with the greatest young people high schools and colleges had to offer. They invaded our lives, our ministry, and our hearts.

And now, though weary from the action-packed summer, we were reluctant to see it end, especially those of us who lived there year-round. We were never ready for this seasonal part of our ministry to grind to a screeching halt. Would this year be different?

My answer came that night, soon after we watched the taillights of the last bus round the corner. We remaining few staff members were working in the kitchen, scrubbing, stacking, and storing the pots and pans for the winter, when our talented cook beckoned, "Take a break! Come eat!"

She didn't have to ask *us* twice! We never ceased to marvel at the palatable creations she concocted with the last of the leftovers from the freezer. Truly a gift.

As the wind whipped and howled outside, we were thankful for the blessing of shelter and the warmth of fellowship. We chatted and chuckled over tales of summer and bowls of steaming food. God was so good!

I had just sipped some creamy, hot soup, when a soft knock and a tentative voice came from outside the kitchen door.

"Hallo! May vee come in?"

> I inched open the door to find a middle-aged couple huddled together against the blustery weather.

I inched open the door to find a middle-aged couple huddled together against the blustery weather. They looked like they could benefit from the warm stove and our chef's concoction, so I quickly ushered them in and pushed the door closed against the wind.

"Forgeev us, vee saw your lights on and . . ."

"Please—have a seat." We pulled up two stools beside the giant oven, so they could come in and thaw out. "If you're hungry, help yourselves to whatever looks good!"

Well, it *all* looked good to them, especially the fresh fruit, which they quickly stuffed in their pockets.

"Thank you!" They wasted no time devouring all the would-be leftovers. Not a word was said while they ate; we just stood staring, as if we'd never seen the north wind blow strange people into our kitchen before.

Mopping up the last bit of soup from her bowl with a chunk of bread, the woman looked up at her captive audience and smiled ever so sweetly.

"My name ees Valentina, and dees ees my husband Alexander—vee call heem Sasha."

They had flown from their homeland, Ukraine, and were supposed to stay with a sponsor family for several weeks. But due to communication glitches, they ended up with no sponsor family, no place to stay, no food, and no money. Our hearts went out to these weary travelers.

I glanced at Sasha, a seemingly gentle man. He sat quietly, smiling cordially and nodding occasionally as we talked, but said little.

Valentina, on the other hand, spoke readily, with a delightful Slavic accent. We asked what brought them to Manitou.

"Sasha, he ees vell known in Ukraine for hees artvork." Valentina gazed at her husband with a look of deep admiration, almost reverence.

"Vee come so he can vork in gallery, doing many artvorks for special exhibition *just* for *heem*, in December. Den vee go home."

Wow, a renowned artist in our midst! Perhaps he'd show us his work sometime. But for now, they needed more than a fan club; they needed a comfortable place to stay. So while they finished their meal, our staff busily prepared a place for them to stay: cabin #15. I was thrilled to have new "neighbors" next door to my cabin, #14, even if for a short while.

God gave us memorable moments as Valentina and I cultivated a special friendship. While Sasha worked long hours at the gallery, she would come into my office, usually just sitting near my desk while I worked. As autumn tiptoed into winter, I realized the unique ministry opportunity we'd been given. Each time they expressed their gratitude to us, we were quick to point them to the *Lord's* hand of blessing. But they remained unresponsive to any mention of God.

Nonetheless, God graciously continued to enrich our lives through each other. Our casual conversations in cabin and car often took unexpected detours—morphing into riveting history, poli-sci, and geography lessons. Valentina talked of the radical changes taking place in their beloved homeland. Less than a year earlier, Ukraine had become its own independent country when the Soviet Union dissolved.

God Is Eternal

Her words somehow breathed new life into the dry college-textbook pages of my mind. Words like *Ukrainian SSR, Bolsheviks, Red Army,* and *Holodor famine of 1932* were no longer cold facts on a European-history exam. Now they had faces and names and personalities—and I was beginning to see that with fresh changes had come fresh fears.

I listened intently as Valentina expressed their fears. Growing up in that time and place was hard, yes, but it's all that any of them had known since 1917. Now everything was different. Scary. Who could they trust? What did the future hold for their children and their grandchildren? When would peace be guaranteed?

Valentina was a wealth of intriguing information, animated and adorable.

And Sasha? Each time I visited the art gallery, I found this quiet, gifted man diligently laboring over another creative "vork"— I was especially impressed with the lithographs, so Sasha gave me a spontaneous Art Appreciation 101 course, humbly demonstrating his craft.

I wondered how much of his quiet demeanor was shyness and how much was simply a language and cultural barrier. I prayed that God would show me.

His answer came the very next day, as two exciting thoughts came to mind. A few brief calls led me to a small cluster of Ukrainian folks in the community and a Russian Club at the Air Force Academy. Both groups were anxious to accommodate us the following week. We could hardly wait!

Wednesday night, as soon as we entered the reception room full of Ukrainian men and women, our meek and mild Sasha came to life— his huge grin, congenial conversing, and ready laughter were a sight to behold. I even detected a few joyful tears cascading down his cheeks, as he embraced his new "family" of friends. I didn't understand a word being said all evening, but it didn't matter—I was having the time of my life seeing my friends so happy!

The following Friday night, Valentina and Sasha, decked out in native costume, honored me by being my dinner guests at the Air Force Academy Officers' Club. They had never experienced anything quite so fancy or tasty, and they filled take-home boxes with everything that wasn't nailed to the table. Surely the chef was pleased.

I drove them to their next event—the Russian Club meeting. What an appreciative and attentive audience these young cadets were as their two guests modeled their native garb, presented a fascinating slide show, answered countless questions, and asked a few of their own.

Our memorable times would soon end, as Sasha's "Big Night" drew near: the grand art exhibition, exclusively of his works, in a gallery somewhere downtown. I didn't know the exact date, or place, but was sure they would give me plenty of notice so I could be there to support them.

One Friday evening in December, after working late at the ministry office, I popped the casserole into the oven that I had prepared that morning as a surprise meal for Sasha and Valentina. It was not something I normally did, but I felt led to do it this particular day. Heading out, meal in hand, I glanced at the clock and realized it had taken too long, it was too late—surely they would have eaten by now. So I turned back to my cabin.

But something made me head back down the stairs to cabin #15. Embarrassed, I stood on their porch mentally rehearsing my "I'm-sorry-I know-it's too-late-for-your dinner-tonight-but . . . " apology speech.

Balancing the casserole in one hand, I knocked hesitantly with the other. When the door opened, so did my mouth. But no words came out. There in the doorway stood Valentina in her festive native attire. Beside her was Sasha, fully decked out as well. Behind them, filling the entire room, were Sasha's framed pictures.

"How deed you know to come?" Valentina's face brightened.

God Is Eternal

I had no idea this was Sasha's Big Night—the whole reason the two had come to America! Now, here they were, all dressed and ready . . . and their ride had never arrived. When I heard how soon—and how far away—their show was, I prayed, *Lord, help us!* as we flew into action.

I raced up the hill to get my station wagon, drove it down to the campground, parked it by the curb at the bottom of the hill, and headed by foot up to their cabin. Up and down the steep gravel path we went, scaling the twenty-five or more stone steps each way, racing back and forth, hauling armloads of framed art. I glanced at my watch. No way could we load everything up, drive downtown, and set up in time.

> "How deed you know to come?"
> Valentina's face brightened.

Lord, You are the God of the impossible. Help us, please, I prayed as we huffed and puffed our way uphill and down, our legs and lungs burning. Miraculously, every picture fit into the back of the station wagon, the three of us squeezed into the front, and we were off— armed with Valentina's trusty directions and my silent prayers.

Precious cargo filled my car. Thankfulness filled my heart. I wanted so much for them to see the hand of God in all this and embrace His love. Just then, Valentina asked again:

"How deed you know to come?"

I paused, drew a deep breath, and answered, "*I didn't* know, Valentina."

"You . . . then how . . . why . . ."

"*I* didn't know. But *God* did. He put me on your doorstep at just the right time, and is, this minute, working to get us where we need to be. He cares about you. He's a *good God*, Valentina.

"Oh yes! Good God—*good* God!"

My heart soared. It was the first time either of them had acknowledged God, since day one. Seeds had been planted, biblical truths had been shared, and practical needs had been met. But now my friends had personally, inexplicably experienced the hand of God working behind the scenes on their behalf.

Finally, here we were, unloading and setting up in record time, ready before the first person came! Sasha's beautiful artwork filled the gallery. His evening was a remarkable success.

The stunning lithograph Sasha gave me, signed and framed, reminds me of the gift God gave me that autumn night when the word "Hallo . . . " ushered in a joyous mutual ministry.

Like this quiet artist, God was *silent*. But He was *never still*. Just as Sasha wordlessly but industriously created his masterpieces, God quietly orchestrated His own: ordering events and circumstances, working through people and prayers—faithfully providing, encouraging, blessing, and guiding!

Twice, Sasha and Valentina's disappointments were actually God's *appointments*: when their sponsors, then their ride, opted out, He stepped in.

I thanked the Lord for bringing this endearing couple into my life. From the moment our kitchen door opened up to them that first night, to the moment their cabin door closed behind them for the last time, God was at work. One day may they see it.

Artist, meet the Master. For He is a good God—*good* God, indeed.

God Is Eternal

God Is Strong

A Close Encounter

Sudha Khristmukti

I'd lost my best and closest friend, and I was reeling from the pain. The fact that I would never see her again filled me with despair. To add to this, suddenly a chemical imbalance in my brain thrust me into a severe depression that tore away my sense of self.

I felt like I was constantly in the eye of a storm raging around me.

The smooth functioning of my life and plans had been disrupted completely. I didn't know how to cope. It was too overwhelming to bear.

I cried, "Why me, Lord?" a thousand times, but He seemed distant and silent.

"Where are you, Lord, when I need you the most? Are you even there?" I begged in frustration and anguish. I was very young then— and so was my faith. What was I supposed to do when God didn't listen? And even if He did hear me, would He care to answer? I began questioning my newfound faith.

To uplift my state of mind and heart, I started cycling and swimming. I'd get on my blue bicycle at early dawn, pushing myself beyond my despondent feelings, and then I'd bike eight kilometers to the swimming pool. Besides being good exercise and relaxation, this gave me some quiet time before a busy day unfurled and engulfed me.

The swimming pool was outdoors, surrounded by a belt of tall coconut trees. That particular morning, I'd reached the pool way before dawn, and it was very dark. I could even see faint stars in the sky above. The beautiful moon was still out and cast its silver light around the pool area. I always enjoyed watching this tranquil scene while backstroking, so I didn't turn on the pool lights. Pool lights, I thought, can never match nature's magic.

As I was about to dive into the deep end as usual, I suddenly felt a presence behind me, as if a person were gently but firmly holding me back. I teetered on the edge of the board, wondering if I was going to fall, but I caught my balance. I turned around, expecting an unexpected early swimmer to be there.

> I suddenly felt a presence behind me, as if a person were gently but firmly holding me back.

There was no one.

But there had to be someone there! What was the strong presence I had felt behind me? Who had held me back?

Who on earth was it? I knew I was totally alone. The pool caretaker had given me keys so I could use the place as the earliest arrival. I had opened the locked premises myself. No one else could have gotten in.

As I pondered this strange phenomenon, I was compelled to carefully look into the pool.

I shuddered.

There was absolutely not a drop of water in the pool.

All I could see were the blue tiles, twenty-two feet below, where I had been about to dive headfirst.

I began to tremble as the reality of the situation hit me.

I could not even begin to imagine the consequences had I dived. No one would have arrived for at least three hours, which was when a few regular swimmers would start trickling in. By then the stars would have disappeared and the sun would be rising.

God Is Strong

I trembled in awe and shock with the sudden realization that I definitely would have either been killed or left completely paralyzed had I survived.

I felt numbed and dazed. And nauseated.

After a while I was jolted wide awake with a new and amazing enlightenment: God *did* care about me, about what happened to me! In fact, His care was too deep for me to fathom.

He was watching over me, protecting me, through the ministering of His angels, and I hadn't even been aware of it! How many other times had He shielded me from unknown dangers, without my knowledge?

I had thought God didn't care about my loss, my suffering. I had felt abandoned by Him.

God knew how much I needed Him to reach out to me, to assure me that He cared even when I thought He didn't. He knew the only way I would be touched was through something tangible—an experience that I would have to undoubtedly believe.

Through this experience, I was able to fully grasp the meaning and truth in the promise of Psalm 91:11: "He orders his angels to protect you wherever you go."

And Psalm 91:4: "His faithful promises are your armor and protection."

How often had I read these verses! But never was I so deeply and personally touched as now.

Who else but the living Lord would care to let me know beyond doubt of His divine help, divine presence?

No matter where I am, no matter what my condition—His love and care remain permanent and unchanging in the face of life's changes.

That blessed assurance is forever mine. And I cling to it every day.

God Is Good

GOD'S FINGERPRINTS

Karen Morerod

"God, I know you're there. It's just been so long since I've seen evidence that you are active in my life. I want to see something that I know is you—something with your autograph." After a few more tears, my prayer was done.

It was one of those *Can you hear me now?* spiritual seasons of my life. I was having regular times of prayer, but everything seemed dry. I needed guidance on some pressing issues, and nothing seemed to be happening. So, at that point, any sign that God was really hearing me would be the spiritual encouragement I needed. I wasn't looking for some great miracle, just comfort that I wasn't alone.

Several weeks later, while I was driving home from the store, my cell phone rang. "Mrs. Morerod, this is the police department. I am at your house, and it has been broken into."

"What? You're kidding!" I stammered to ask more questions, but my mind swirled with: *When? How?* And, *Oh no, my new laptop!*

The police officer continued, "We have suspects in custody and, we think, most of your belongings." Now *that* was a different story.

"I will be there in ten minutes," I informed the officer.

I tried to create the story with the little information I had. How could they already have a suspect in custody? The house had only been unoccupied for a couple of hours. Were they watching the house? What did the thieves take?

But the most important issue at the moment was that the police had our property. "Thank you, God. I can't believe this. Thank you! Thank you!" I declared aloud in the car.

Confusion and gratefulness ran together as I remembered years earlier when our home had been broken into. Of the few things missing, nothing was ever recovered, and no one was ever apprehended.

Again I blurted aloud, "This is such a God thing. Thank you!"

The police officer met me in the yard as I arrived home. "Don't touch anything as you enter the house. We will take fingerprints later, and we don't want those prints messed up."

> I wasn't looking for some great miracle,
> just comfort that I wasn't alone.

Still on my high that our belongings were recovered, I wasn't prepared for the scene I walked into. Drawers dumped out. Doors hung open. Computers, phones, printers, and wires lay in a jumbled mess on the floor in our study. Jewelry-box contents along with the contents of our closet and dresser littered the bedroom floor. The scene looked as if a tornado had been unleashed inside the walls of our home. Previous break-ins had never involved this level of ransacking.

"Look at this mess," I ranted, quickly forgetting my elation. "This is crazy! Can they come back and clean up the mess they made?"

I tried some humor to maintain my composure about the situation, but each demolished room I entered caused more anger.

After my shock and exasperation over the condition of the house, I asked, "So how did you catch these guys?"

"This is the weirdest thing. It's such a fluke," the officer began.

"Our police captain was off duty today, attending a yearly training event. He was on his way home for lunch and noticed a black SUV pulled over to the side of the road just a couple of miles from here. He stopped to see if they needed help. As he approached the car, he noticed some suspicious property inside. He started going through the stuff and found papers and other items with different peoples' names and addresses. He found one item with your address. He detained the men in the car and radioed for me to check this address. Of course when I got here, I saw your house had been broken into."

The officer laughed again, "This is such a fluke. The captain is never going to let us live this down. We officers are the ones who are supposed to catch things like this. I just can't believe how weird this is."

"This isn't a fluke," I immediately replied. "I don't know if you believe in God, but this is a God thing."

The comment seemed to go over his head. But my heart knew God was involved. Even so, as I stood in the rubble the thieves had left behind, I didn't remember my prayer of several weeks prior.

The detective on the scene came into the room. "We need to go to the crime vehicle and identify your belongings." We drove the several miles to the site.

The police ushered me to the passenger side of a black SUV. A variety of items littered the inside of the car. The officer pulled one item out at a time, and I identified our property.

Back at the house, the officer who had stayed to watch the house came out the door to leave. "Boy, I'm never going to forget this. You guys are so lucky." And again said, "This whole thing has been such a stroke of luck."

By this time, several other detectives arrived with the fingerprint kit. "This will be messy, but we feel we have a good case here. We

God Is Good

just want some fingerprints to put these men here at the scene of the break-in."

He showed me one such print. "See here?" he said pointing to the door. "You can see where they kicked the door in. We have a good shoe print and will compare it to the suspect's shoe."

Within a few hours, most of our identified belongings were brought back to the house. We gladly took possession of them. The officers left, leaving black fingerprinting dust in various areas of the house.

Later that day, with soapy water, I cleaned black dust from the door, some spots upstairs, and in our family room. I reflected on my limited knowledge of fingerprinting technology. *Would they be able to get good enough prints? Would they match the men's who were driving the SUV?*

> In all the excitement of the day,
> I hadn't stopped to make the connection.

Suddenly I remembered my prayer from weeks earlier, my prayer that God would *show up* somehow for me to see His autograph. In all the excitement of the day, I hadn't stopped to make the connection.

"God, thank you for working in this whole event. This whole thing was not just a coincidence." Then as I continued cleaning off fingerprinting dust, I laughed aloud, "God, it's *Your* prints that are all over this scene!"

Amusing myself further, I wondered what God's fingerprints would look like and if mere police detectives could recognize them. I knew that was pure imagination, but it caused me to turn to God again, in a new and thankful way.

For weeks after and even now when I think about it, I realize my thankfulness is multidimensional. Yes, I am grateful that our belongings were recovered. But it was done in such a way that I know it wasn't just a "fluke." God's fingerprints were evident in the whole situation.

Was I happy about cleaning up the mess left by the perpetrators? Was I pleased they left scratches on my computer screen? Am I glad we have to buy a new doorframe and trim? No!

But I learned that when I ask God for a sign, He can be most creative. I am grateful for the reminder that God still hears and is concerned about me. And He *wants* to be found by us as Proverbs 8:17 says: "I love all who love me. Those who search will surely find me."

God's fingerprints are amazing!

God Is Protector

COME HELL OR HIGH WATER

Mimi Greenwood Knight

*W*hen I was growing up in South Louisiana in the seventies, a hurricane brewing in the Gulf meant nothing more to me and my eleven brothers and sisters than the potential for adventure. The excitement included days off school, a visit from our Gulf Coast cousins, sleeping bags on the floor, no baths or bedtimes, hours spent by candlelight listening to the grown-ups reminisce, and ice cream for breakfast ("Quick! Before it melts with the electricity off").

We loved hurricanes the way northern kids love snow days, never understanding the very real danger, because we were surrounded by grown-ups who were good at hiding whatever fear they may have felt. My parents and aunts and uncles centered their lives on us kids, and we knew it. It never dawned on us that anything could actually harm us—not even a hurricane. Our parents wouldn't allow it.

All our lives we'd heard about the "Big One" hitting New Orleans someday, but it never seemed like a reality. It was a ghost story the big people told us just as their parents had told them, right up there with California falling into the ocean. In our minds hurricanes destroyed coastal areas, and we were sitting pretty an hour inland—whispering in the dark as the winds whipped and our parents scurried about lighting candles and gathering water. If we begged hard enough, we might even be allowed to venture out during the eye of the storm to listen to the eerie silence.

I loved going to the store with my mother and aunts before a storm to pick up last-minute supplies, loved eavesdropping on the grownups as they swapped survival tips. The air was electric, and natural social barriers were forgotten, with strangers chatting like old friends. Neighbors we hardly ever saw stopped by our house to see if we needed anything.

The few times a storm really did look threatening, my siblings, cousins, and I thrilled to see our usually stalwart parents come unglued—just a bit. I loved every exhilarating minute before, during, and after a Louisiana hurricane.

Now, thirty years later, my husband, David, and I are the ones protecting our four kids from the anxiety of South Louisiana hurricane season. They're the ones safe in the knowledge that we'd never allow any storm to harm one hair on their heads.

On August 28, 2005, as we prepared for a visit from Hurricane Katrina, I easily slipped into the pattern my parents, aunts, and uncles had raised me in, going about storm preparations with an air of everyday calm. If I was scared, my kids wouldn't know it.

Katrina developed so fast that when David left his office in New Orleans on Friday afternoon, it seemed like any other day. There was no sign that something big was about to happen there on Monday. By Sunday, though, the weather reports looked ominous. I thought about the last two times we'd evacuated only to have the storm change course and pass us by. Evacuating four kids, two adults, and three dogs is no small feat. Plus, with everyone else evacuating, where would we go?

I felt calm about staying. I called our family on the Mississippi Gulf Coast and invited them to ride it out with us the way our Gulf Coast cousins had so many times—all those great memories—then started battening down the hatches.

God Is Protector

Our kids knew the drill as well as we did at their age: Gather candles, flashlights, and battery-operated radios to a central location. Stash bikes, barbeque grills, and other loose objects in the garage. Call the neighbors to see who's leaving and who'll be riding it out with us. Buy plenty of ice. Just before the storm, fill all the bathtubs with water for potty flushing. Loss of electricity is a given and, since we live in the country with our own well, no electricity means no water. I could feel that old excitement building.

Twice, my thirteen-year-old daughter, Molly, asked if maybe we should evacuate, but by then her own Gulf Coast cousins had arrived and the hurricane party was in full swing. To three-year-old Jonah it was one big slumber party. Nine-year-old Hewson showed definite

Katrina arrived at our house early Monday morning and lasted for nine terrifying hours.

signs of being a hurricane groupie like his mama. And fifteen-year-old Haley's only regret was loss of privacy since we'd declared her attic bedroom off limits during the storm.

When the schools closed, I felt like a third grader again, excited to know we'd be having ice cream for breakfast and brewing coffee on the barbeque grill. I remembered gathering downed limbs from the yard with my cousins, as my dad and uncles cooked breakfast over the backyard grill, laughing and one-upping one another with stories.

I was eight years old again and ready for the next hurricane party. The last thing I did before I went to bed Sunday night was email my brothers up north: "I hope y'all have fond memories of New Orleans, because after tomorrow, the Crescent City as we know it may not exist." I didn't mean it. I was being dramatic.

Katrina arrived at our house early Monday morning and lasted for nine terrifying hours. Through ceiling to floor windows we watched mammoth oaks get sucked out of the ground like saplings. Eighty percent of the pine forest around our house disappeared.

Our garage was flattened, our back deck smashed. The tin roof above our heads rippled and flapped. David's truck, tractor, our old pump house, and the barn all disappeared under mounds of trees. A window exploded, sending missiles of broken glass flying two rooms away. The plate glass that covers two walls in our living room heaved in and out as if the whole room were breathing. *If it goes*, I thought, *there's no place to hide from the glass.*

We had bought this house because we loved the windows and trees. Now it seemed that the combination would be the death of us.

Miraculously, though, all but one window stayed intact. Hundreds of trees fell around us, reminding me of a giant game of pick-up sticks. Yet it was as if God had drawn a line around the house where we huddled and prayed—not a single tree was allowed to hit us.

More than once during the storm, I noticed the kids searching my face to ascertain if they should be scared, yet I felt unexplainably calm. We hunkered in the hall, sang songs, and told stories. When the wind finally stopped and we ventured outside, it was dusk.

Our eight acres looked like a bomb had gone off. We found out later that our area had been hit by hundreds of tornadoes that spun off of the hurricane. The devastation stretched for miles. The "Big One" had finally come. We were thankful that we had been on its weaker side.

As we dealt with the aftermath of the storm—hacking our way through the trees to civilization, searching for family and friends, good news, bad news, the uncertainty of David's job, the loss of mine, and the monthlong exile before our home was repaired enough for us to return to it—I came to a realization. As much as I was there to calm my kids' fears, in truth, it had worked the other way around.

God Is Protector

They were the ones who kept me grounded. When I told them things like, "All of this is just stuff. None of it matters. If we lose this house, we'll build another one," I was talking to myself.

When I assured them the storm couldn't last much longer, that we'd be able to return home soon, that the important thing was knowing all our loved ones were alive, I mostly assured myself.

This is one family who won't be riding out another hurricane. When we hear about a sizable storm heading our way, we move further inland. Still, this experience has become part of us, part of who we are. It's shown us what really matters in life. We've discovered things about ourselves and the people who love us that we might never have known. We've been touched, amazed, and humbled by the generosity and love of friends, family, and strangers alike.

And through it all, God showed me a secret about those big people who built a fortress around us for so many years. During the turbulent times in life, it's kids who keep their parents afloat—not the other way around.

God Is Truthful

GOD SUPPLIED THE WORDS

Timothy Burns

"God, I have no idea what to say. Josh and I haven't talked, really talked, in over four years, and the last time I went out of my way to spend time with him, he only complained about how difficult I am to get along with. God, I need you here. I don't know what to do."

As I waited on my ex-wife's front porch, I gazed back, over the past five turbulent years. Gazed? Grieved was more accurate. Divorce is always hard, but when five kids are involved, it's especially difficult. Every child gets hit differently by the trauma of divorcing parents. My oldest son Josh internalized the pain.

The court had dealt my kids like a deck of cards into different homes, and Josh had stayed close to his mom. He wouldn't come to the door when I picked up his younger siblings for visitation weekends. When she moved two hours away for a new job, my relationship with him collapsed completely.

Standing on the porch in the warm July sunshine, grief gripped the place in my heart where the joy over my family once flourished. The events of the past five years weren't pleasant snapshots. The image of what I'd wanted in a family had crashed to the floor, shattered by my ex's and my inability to make our marriage work. Like a broken mirror, each shard reflected a piece of the family I once had: colors from birthday party balloons, my daughter's first pink dress, band concerts, and family dinners.

Each sliver caught part of the whole, and now they cut my emotional fingers as I tried to pick them up and look into that past again. I knew that the fractured pieces would never be put together again.

"Hi, Dad." Josh swung the door open, blinking as he stepped into the light.

"Hey, Josh. How are you?"

"Okay. What do you want to do?"

"I don't know. Have you had lunch yet?"

"No."

"How about heading toward the mall? We can find someplace to eat."

What does a dad say to his oldest and firstborn son when he hasn't seen him for much more than a few minutes at a time over five years? I never have been gifted at small talk. According to my kids, I was even worse at showing interest in what was important to them.

I can only imagine what Josh and I must have looked like as we stood awkwardly on the porch. A couple of strangers staring at the concrete? Definitely not father and son.

My ex-wife and I had separated when Josh was in tenth grade. She moved away as his junior year began. I did my best to stay in touch, but Josh always had something else to do when I came to visit. I always tried to attend Josh's school plays, but those weren't times to connect. I watched as part of the audience, and when the play was over, Josh would wave from across the auditorium and disappear with his friends.

Josh found his creative outlet in school plays. Although he didn't apply much energy to his studies, his talent on stage was 4.0. He carried a lead in *Guys and Dolls* and a minor lead in other productions.

On the other hand, I'd never ventured onto a stage. Instead I competed in sports, edited the school yearbook, and found my identity in competition—which taught me little about building relationships with my young kids. Josh and I were two different people with different interests. We had little in common to talk about.

The spring of his senior year, magic happened. The Young Americans Performing Arts School found Josh, and he discovered a reason to graduate and go on to college. Josh spent the next two years learning the performing arts and performing around the world. On both U.S. coasts, in Germany, England, and Poland, Josh learned and taught younger students the performing arts. Concurrently, the cast learned what it took to build a performing-arts career. The tours required investing in and caring for others, managing shows, and maintaining positive relationships along with stage performances.

Josh flourished like a cornfield in July. Unfortunately, we still spent only ten to fifteen minutes together a few times a year, usually after a show that was within driving distance. The chasm between us grew.

Almost an hour had passed since I'd picked him up. We were well into our meals, while the conversation still nibbled appetizers. I didn't know my son anymore, and I couldn't find my way through the wall between us. He recited a summary of the past tours and the kids he had met. We talked about what the next year might hold and how my business still wasn't solvent. As the last bit of small talk dissolved into an uncomfortable silence, I looked down at my cold burrito and wondered what to say next.

God met me there. I had nothing, and my God supplied His perfect provision. A question broke the silence in my mind. I knew this was God's answer to my prayer and His supply to our relationship crisis.

"Josh, what do you think that I think of your time in the Young Americans?"

God Is Truthful

His chin fell, and his voice quivered. We had never discussed his career choice. He hesitated; I suspected he didn't want to expose his heart and risk ridicule.

"Dad, I think that you think I am wasting my time. I think that you think I am squandering my talents and that I should be in a regular college, getting a regular degree."

I sat in stunned silence as the words fell to the floor. Actually, as I had watched my son pursue his love of the performing arts over the past four years, my admiration had grown. I knew that one key to a satisfying career path is to pursue your passion. I also knew I hadn't yet connected with my passion, at least one that would pay.

As a traveling arts college, YA is one of the pure apprenticeship programs in the nation. The cast and crew learn the business side of performing as they hone their performance skills. The group transforms the student body when they visit, and behind them a metamorphosis in artistic beauty takes place.

> Yet in my absence from his life, Josh was haunted by fear of a harsh dad's continuing disapproval.

Josh's love of performing had been evident since preschool. He had found the perfect fit. I marveled at his talent, his spirit, and the gifts he was bestowing on those he taught. Yet in my absence from his life, Josh was haunted by fear of a harsh dad's continuing disapproval.

For the next half hour, God allowed me to pour into Josh the blessing that sons need from their dads. I told him how proud I was of his achievements. I encouraged him to pursue his dream. Our conversation gave him permission to live his dream and not to think that I expected him to pursue mine.

We also talked about how hard it had been for me after our family dissolved. I had been absent from his life in most ways, and I wanted him to see that it wasn't because I disapproved of him, but because I was unable to process the grief of losing our family. I remembered attending his graduation open house at his mom's. I came with a small gift and then left suddenly. He told me that this made him feel he was unimportant. But the truth was that I hadn't been able to suppress the grief I'd felt over losing track of three years of his life.

I don't think I finished my burrito. Tears stained our faces and plates, and I don't like soggy Mexican food. But I do remember the next few hours we spent together. We talked, went to a movie, and for the first time in five years spent father and son time together.

That afternoon together was a turning point for both of us. Josh became a leader and stage director within the YA community. He now is a world-class dance instructor, directing his own dance company on the West Coast. And I began to let go of the grief and regret that had kept me away from my son.

In one of our recent conversations, Josh said that when he made room for God in his professional life, opportunities evolved that he could never have accomplished on his own. "Now I need a personal life, so I can let Him in there too."

Jesus reminded his listeners about the fifth commandment (see Mark 10:19), and Paul quoted the entire command in Ephesians 6:2–3: "'Honor your father and mother.' This is the first commandment with a promise. If you honor your father and mother, 'Things will go well for you, and you will have a long life on the earth.'"

I've learned that this principle isn't only about a child's responsibility toward his or her parents. It is also about a parent's responsibility to bless his or her children and be an example of love. Even when we don't know how to do this on our own, thankfully, God provides the wisdom we need.

God Is Truthful

God Is Mighty

GOD AND MY "SIDEKICK"

Dianne Daniels

*C*rack!

As the solid plank of pine broke in two, a wall of fear and self-doubt crumbled to pieces inside of me, reminding me of the day I embarked on this adventure.

"You signed up for *what*?" With tones of shock and a sense of absurdity, my husband, parents, and friends all voiced the same question.

"Tae Kwon Do," I answered. "You know, like karate."

Those closest to me tried not to laugh at the image of me kicking and punching around the room in white pajamas. They probably thought this was yet another one of my crazy ideas that would last about a month before I slunk away in embarrassment.

No one had ever called me an athlete. As a child, I enjoyed playing sports, but never performed particularly well. Let's just say my trophy case was a bit heavy on *participation* ribbons. This didn't bother me, though. My favorite thing about sports was being with my friends.

But when I reached adulthood, I realized I was not in touch with my body. I felt out of balance. Friends would say they could feel when they were getting sick. Others recognized the exact moment they got pregnant. When it came to my physical being, every hiccup caught me off guard.

I felt God calling me to take action and correct this situation. So when a coupon for a local karate school came in the mail, I marched in and signed on the dotted line. The girl behind the counter gave me a uniform and pointed out an instructor. "Tell him you're new today," the girl said. I did as I was told, and the instructor introduced me to the class.

Did the other students notice my jaw drop as I realized I was possibly the only person in the room who had driven herself to class? I had been told that the children had a separate program at this school. Apparently teenagers did not qualify as children, because here they all stood, looking as if they were wondering why this old lady was invading their class.

We started with stretching, and as I looked at the juvenile rubber bands around me, I cursed myself for not bending over in the past ten years. After stretching, everyone dropped to their knees, closed their eyes, and remained silent for a minute or two. I had no idea what they were doing, but this seemed like the perfect time for a quick prayer.

God, please watch over me. This whole karate thing seemed like a good idea, but now I am not so sure. I think You brought me here for a reason. Could You please let me know what it is? And could You please make sure that I do okay and don't get hurt or too humiliated? Please?

When quiet time was over, we started doing the moves I expected. I watched myself in the mirror as I kicked and punched according to the instructor's directions.

Hey, I'm not too bad at this! This is fun! I didn't know I could kick this high. In fact, I didn't know I could kick without falling over.

Before long, I forgot how young the other students were. Grouped by belt color, everyone in the class had started within the last month or two. Plus, the second time I went to class, another adult was there. He and I became fast friends amid the school-aged crowd.

God Is Mighty

Twice a week I went to learn new self-defense techniques and patterns of putting different moves together. As my abilities grew, so did my sense of self. For the first time in my life, I was aware of how long my arms were and how far I could reach. I knew how strong my legs were and how high I could kick without losing my balance. I learned how quickly I could move, turn, and duck. Most important, I learned how to link my brain with the rest of my body. I had always been "quick on my feet" when it came to *talking* my way out of situations. Now I was *literally* quick on my feet.

> I became keenly aware that He had brought me here because He did not want my mind disconnected from my body any longer.

My favorite part of Tae Kwon Do continued to be the moment of quiet at the beginning of class. I used this time to pray and focus my mind on God. I became keenly aware that He had brought me here because He did not want my mind disconnected from my body any longer. He wanted me to be a whole, intact person whom He could use. I prayed for His protection, His strength, and His courage as each class brought new challenges. While I found I was better at this sport than I thought I would be, it was still scary. Practicing kicks and punches in the mirror was fun. Putting on pads and practicing on people terrified me. And worse was having people practice on me!

Thankfully, I made it through the first month without injury. I was having a great time. I always left class with a smile on my face. But one day, that changed. As the other students filed out of the room at the end of our session, the instructor pulled me aside and said, "I think you will be ready to test next month."

"Test?" I was happy as a white belt. Who needed more?

"At the test you'll have to break a board," he said. "We'll start working on that next time."

Next time? I suddenly wasn't so sure there would be a next time. I wasn't really a board-breaking kind of woman. Boards were meant for building decks or for use as paneling inside saunas. They really didn't deserve to be broken.

Besides, the people I had seen breaking boards on television were huge, muscular, sweaty men with bandanas wrapped around their heads. That definitely wasn't me. Plus, I was pretty sure that forcing any part of my body through a solid piece of wood could hurt. I didn't believe in hurting myself on purpose.

Despite my resistance, I felt a funny twinge deep in the pit of my stomach. It was excitement. I knew God was telling me I could step out of my comfort zone once again and try something even scarier. I went home and told my husband that I was going to test for my yellow belt and break a board.

"Wow," he said.

At the next class, the instructor told me I should use my strongest skill to break my first board. We agreed that I would do a step-behind sidekick. He got out a pad that was slightly bigger than the board would be and I practiced kicking the center of it. This practice brought about a new fear. What if I kicked the instructor's fingers while he held the board? This was another thing to pray about.

When testing day finally arrived, I awoke with a knot in my stomach. A panel of judges would evaluate me in three different areas. I would do the required kicks and punches with a group of students. Then I would put them together into a routine, called a form. Finally, I would face the board.

As I drove to the test, I asked God to stay close by my side. Despite my faithful practice, I felt unprepared for the challenge. What if I made a mistake and embarrassed myself in front of strangers? What if

God Is Mighty

I missed the board and kicked the instructor? What if I actually *broke* the board and passed the test? What would they expect me to do in yellow belt class?

"God, this is crazy! How can I be afraid of success *and* failure at the same time? I need your strength and your courage. Please let me feel Your presence today." My prayers came from the bottom of my heart.

> "How can I be afraid of success *and* failure at the same time?"

Each stage of the test went well, although I felt a little silly doing my form all by myself with nearly one hundred teenaged eyes watching me, along with the ten eyes of the judges. In spite of my discomfort, however, I could feel the crowd pulling for me. When I finished, everyone applauded, and as I turned from the judges toward the audience, the smiles I saw told me I had a new family.

This encouraging support did not, however, change the fact that board breaking still loomed ahead. As I stepped into position, I realized the soles of my feet were probably as sweaty as my palms. Would I leave a footprint on the board?

I looked at the instructor holding the piece of wood and prayed that I wouldn't kick him. *God, please don't let me get hurt. But above all, don't let me hurt anyone else.*

As I prayed, I felt an overwhelming sense of God's presence fill my body. My fears melted away as an unfamiliar strength grew in my muscles. My hands stopped shaking. My breathing slowed. I felt powerful and in control of my body.

"You can do this," the instructor told me. "Visualize yourself kicking something on the other side of the board and go right through it."

So I did.

I felt instant exhilaration. Every one of my prayers was answered—I didn't get hurt, I didn't hurt anyone else, I didn't make a fool of myself, and I felt a new sense of acceptance among my teenage classmates.

And best of all, I knew my mind and body were connected. I felt confident to take on whatever challenge God had for me in the future. I didn't need to worry about how He would use me—I knew I was capable.

God empowered me to take a risk and trust His outcome. Through this step of faith, I saw Him perform a mighty work in me as my confidence and sense of self blossomed. And I have the broken board to prove it.

God Is Mighty

God Is Faithful

A CAMOUFLAGED ANSWER

Steven Thompson

My heart rate elevated as the cold tires rumbled over the desolate blacktop. An occasional ribbon of fine drifting snow snaked across the road, and dancing fumes from the car's exhaust reminded me of the subzero temp.

The harsh weather magnified the financial crisis I was facing. I couldn't sense God that bleak February morning, even though I had constantly pleaded with Him for deliverance.

The crisis began with a childhood dream. I had always wanted to become a farmer like my dad. I took my first steps toward that dream before I graduated from high school. Dad was renting several farms and graciously let me assume the responsibility for one.

During my senior year of high school, I awoke every morning at five a.m. to care for my livestock, and after school I returned to do chores again. Then I'd work till midnight in the fields before retiring. Despite the long hours and heavy labor, I felt a deep romance for farming.

An unexpected roadblock arose two years later when Dad and I lost the leases on the land we rented. We began looking for a new opportunity in agriculture. My parents and I coinvested in a farming operation in a community eighty miles from where we lived.

Starting a joint business wasn't easy. Dad and I didn't always share the same business philosophies. Eventually we split our partnership, and I took sole ownership of our hog operation.

By my midtwenties two major events began to reshape my life. First I entered a relationship with Jesus Christ. I soon learned that the Holy Spirit would guide me, even in my business ventures, and I often sought His council.

A year later I met a beautiful brunette, and within months we married, which changed the configuration of my life and finances from when I had been single, I hadn't needed much money, but now that I had a wife, I searched for a stable income and accepted a minimum-wage, forty-hour-a-week job.

Shortly after the birth of our first two children, I was given added responsibilities at work, and church activities drew my time away from my business venture. On top of that, higher production costs and lower livestock prices led to a great financial strain. I decided to abandon my business.

Though I felt a distinct leading from God to sell the business quickly, I stubbornly held on. A sharp decline in hog prices added to our mounting debt, and I reluctantly realized that if I didn't sell, we were headed for financial collapse.

The receipts from the sale of livestock didn't come close to covering our debts, and during the next couple of years, I dodged the twenty-some creditors I still owed money to. Since I lived in a small town, I often crossed the street rather than face one of them on the sidewalk.

Though I worked at maintaining a relationship with God, I was frustrated with what I viewed as His lack of interest in my financial problem. Despite my two years of pleading for deliverance, our bills grew. It seemed impossible to pay off several thousand dollars of debt when I received minimum wage. Only a miracle from God could save us, yet He seemed uninterested.

Then the morning of reckoning arrived. I was working second shift at a factory, and when I arrived home about 11:30 p.m., my frustrated wife greeted me. One of my creditors had called her that day, and the conversation had upset her. I knew I had to face the man the next morning. So on that cold February morning, I asked my wife to pray with me before I set out to face the creditor. How could I possibly pay the bill, having barely enough money to meet our family's needs?

I was frustrated with what I viewed as God's lack of interest in my financial problem.

When I sat facing the manager of a grain elevator where I had once purchased feed for the livestock, I expected a lecture since I owed him four hundred dollars. Focusing his eyes on me, he firmly but gently reminded me of the obligations I had been ignoring. He then surprised me by offering a payment plan, letting me pay as little as ten dollars a week. I graciously accepted his proposal.

I decided to contact a couple of other lenders on the way home. Stopping to see our insurance agent, I offered to pay him ten dollars a week on another overdue bill. Finally I stopped at our local hospital where we still owed a few hundred on the delivery of our last child.

I again offered a weekly payment that was minimal compared to our bill. But the woman I talked with cautioned me to make the payment every two weeks (rather than weekly), stating she would rather have me make an arrangement we could afford than to miss a payment. I sensed that God had intervened through her, and in time I discovered that her wisdom had stopped me from overcommitting.

Driving toward home, I felt a sense of relief from years of guilt. But I still had one problem. I had made these commitments in faith—our current budget was actually so tight that I didn't have the resources to fulfill the promises. I knew God wanted me to face our creditors and make an effort to meet our obligations, but I reminded Him that I needed the resources to pay them.

As I continued toward home, an idea arose. The plant where I was employed purchased hundreds of wood pallets every week, and I knew a businessman who had a pile of discarded lumber. I stopped that afternoon to ask the man if I could possibly buy some of his used lumber. He offered it to me free if I kept the area cleaned up.

I arrived home telling my wife of the promises I had made and quickly got ready for work. But I still had to approach the plant manager to see if he would purchase pallets from me. He was open to the idea, and soon I was selling the plant a couple of dozen pallets a week, which supplied the money to fulfill my pledges. It was rewarding to see the bills dwindle.

After we paid off the first three creditors, we began working on other overdue bills. Small miracles surfaced as we struggled to overcome our debt. Once an anonymous gift of money arrived in the mail to help us pay off a commitment we couldn't meet. Two creditors graciously waved interest charges even though we hadn't requested it. At other times, money came from unexpected sources to meet payments.

> I had made these commitments in faith—our current budget was actually so tight that I didn't have the resources to fulfill the promises.

Finally the day came when we were able to dispose of the property, which was our largest debt.

Despite these small miracles, I still wondered why God hadn't provided a larger miracle. He could have enabled us to sell the property early in the crisis for a reasonable profit, which would have cleared up our bills quickly instead of letting us struggle for years to gain financial freedom. Why hadn't the God of miracles delivered us in a more dynamic manner?

But as I went through the process of paying our debts, I searched Scripture for answers. The Scriptures taught me God's principles not only for financial freedom but how to succeed in all of life. God's Word helped me understand that God cared about the crisis I faced, even though I had created it. I was challenged to face my debts and creditors instead of running away from my responsibilities. The Scriptures also taught me about prayer, planning, and persistence. The Bible even gave practical advice on how to guard the successes I would eventually experience.

As time passed, I began to recognize that God had always been present during our financial crisis. He had been the One who prodded me to face our creditors and the One who provided the small miracles along the way. I eventually realized that the greatest benefit from the ordeal hadn't been the financial freedom we eventually gained. The greatest gift was the principles I learned from His Word.

Yes, God had answered my prayer for a grand miracle, but it had arrived in a camouflaged package. Nearly three decades have passed since those grim times, and I still use those principles on a daily basis to face all aspects of my life.

God Is Support

GOD'S BUSINESS PLAN

Lisa Bogart

My to-do list had grown to three pages! I knew starting a business was going to be hard, but the number of details involved shocked me. Thinking about business all the time made my head hurt. Along with wife-and-mommy duties, I'd added entrepreneur. I was trying to go six directions at once and felt exhausted from the effort. Maybe this wasn't such a good idea after all.

When my son entered kindergarten, I thought it was time to find something to do outside the home. I felt the urge to peek out and see what the world had been up to while I had been a stay-at-home mom for five years. I wanted my creative juices to flow in a lucrative direction.

Before staying home with Zach, I had been a graphic designer. Even my hobbies were creative. Needlepoint, scrapbooking, cooking—I found my bliss in making things. Playing with Zach was creative too. We built with Legos, made up stories, colored, painted, cooked, and invented games.

As Zach grew, I found more outlets for my creativity. I made scrapbooks about our family adventures. I created books for Zach to learn his letters, numbers, and opposites. I planned elaborate birthday parties that took a month or two to pull together. I painted T-shirts and knit him sweaters. Each time someone suggested, "You could sell this! Start a business." Really? Which one? Party planner? Scrapbooker?

Knitter? Artist? No way, I did those things for fun. I couldn't start a business. Yet the idea took root.

One day my friend Susan called. "Lisa, would you sell me a pair of your painted T-shirts? Katie was invited to a couple of birthday parties, and your T-shirts would make the perfect gift."

"I suppose. What did you have in mind?"

"Those alphabet ones are so cute. I need 'M is for Melissa' and 'A is for Audrey.' And could you make 'K is for Katie' too. I'll save it for her birthday."

I laughed. "Sure, why not? What sizes do you need?"

"I figure small for all of them."

A week later I heard from Susan again. "The shirts were a hit! Several moms were asking where I got them and wondered if they could order some. Lisa, you've got to do this! Start selling them."

"I can't."

"Yes you can! There's a huge market out there. Go for it!"

Susan kept trying to convince me, and I kept raising objections. "I'm too scared. I don't know anything about running a business. Would anyone really buy my designs?"

> Objections still filled my head,
> but I was intrigued. The idea started to grow.

She tossed off all my fears and encouraged me to try. I hung up the phone. Objections still filled my head, but I was intrigued. The idea started to grow.

Soon I was thinking T-shirts all the time. I doodled ideas. I decided to go for it. But I didn't know which task to tackle first. I knew so little that I didn't even know which person to ask what. I just needed a good product, right? Wrong. I needed to learn the business side of my venture.

I dove into figuring it out. I decided on a name, Tee Party, and I designed my logo. Fun steps. Then I discovered I needed to make sure no one else was doing business as Tee Party. How do you do that? The name had to be registered with the county. I needed to file for a business license. The business expenses were beginning.

Now I needed to open a bank account. All the business finances should to be kept separate from our family accounts. I went to the bank to figure out what I should get. More forms, more decisions, more business know-how to acquire.

Next I needed suppliers. I had to find a place to buy plain T-shirts and sweatshirts at wholesale. I discovered I would need a reseller's license. This would give me the privilege to buy supplies for my business at wholesale prices. Where do I get that kind of license? The State Board of Equalization. I gathered the forms and documents I would need and made a trip to Sacramento. I could have filed online, but if I went in person I could get the license the same day.

With my reseller's license on file, I could now locate suppliers of white goods and fabric markers. One of my favorite craft stores held the answers. When I mentioned to one of the gals what I was trying to find, she said they could sell wholesale to me. Check another detail off the list.

Now, where were all these customers? I decided to gather a focus group. That sounded very business oriented. I made a list of all the friends who had expressed an interest. I came up with a list of thirty gals who were willing to come for a Saturday morning and give me their opinions. And, oh, the opinions they gave. I gained even more business advice.

Have you signed up for small-business classes through continuing education?

Have you joined a service group or networking group to promote your business?

God Is Support

Have you thought about trying specialty-clothing stores?

Have you thought about the catalogue market?

The list of ideas grew and grew. I had a lot of leads to follow up. I wanted to paint shirts and have fun. But it turned out that a business involved a lot more than having a good idea.

So here I was six months in, and I had tracked down all the suggestions. I had my business licenses. I had product samples. I had everything I needed except customers. Now what?

I was frustrated and finally did what I should have done in the first place—I turned to prayer. I sat down in the middle of the living-room floor and poured out my heart to God. *Where are all my customers? I'm supposed to make money, not just pretend to be in business. I don't have the confidence to do this.* I laid it all out—hopes, dreams, fears, the works. And since this was a business conversation, I gave God the bottom line: *I need a concrete answer about what to do next. And I need it soon.*

I peeked open my eyes. Well? What should I do now?

I peeked open my eyes. *Well?* I sat there a little longer. What should I do now? How do I wait to hear from God? I felt better, but I still didn't know what I should do next. I walked into the kitchen. I did the dishes. I cleared off the counters. I answered the phone.

"Hi, Lisa? This is Terry from Celebration Fantastic." Weeks ago I'd sent my T-shirt designs to this national gift catalogue for their consideration.

"Yes. Hello."

"I'm calling to tell you we'd like to feature your personalized kids' Ts and sweatshirts in our fall catalogue."

"Wow! That's great!" Terry went on to give me a lot more

information, but I didn't hear what he said after, "You're in the fall catalogue." My head was so full of whoopee and thank you, God! Happily, Terry would send me a vendor packet of information in the mail. I was too numb to concentrate. I hung up the phone stunned.

I laid out my dreams and fears to God, and forty-five minutes later the phone rang with an answer. I had prayed for my heart's desires before, but I'd never had an answer come so quickly and with such clarity. Prayer doesn't always work like this. God is not a magic genie standing by to grant my every wish. I honestly don't know why this particular time I received an immediate concrete answer, but I do know this experience keeps me closer to God in prayer. I offer God all my details now. I try to start with prayer rather than saving it for the last-ditch plea.

My T-shirt business has come and gone. I learned so much about business and myself in the adventure. The thing I cherish most is the lesson I learned about prayer. Not that God will always, instantly answer my last-ditch, heartfelt prayers of desperation; but He always wants to be involved in every aspect of my life. He is concerned with the very details that drive me to seek Him. I know I can connect with God in prayer at any time. And God listens.

God Is Support

PERFECT TIMING

Pam Morgan

*N*o medication could dull the agony I felt when Kayla, age five, and Alisha, twenty-one months, walked out the door. A car accident had left me quadriplegic, completely paralyzed from the chest down, and for almost two months I had been away from home. I was currently in rehab with no idea when I would be released. I loved seeing my little girls' sweet faces once a week when they visited, but our time together always disappeared too quickly. Watching them leave devastated me.

Usually I managed to stuff the heart-wrenching emotions for Mom's sake—she and my husband, Phil, alternated twenty-four-hour shifts by my side. Yet, truthfully, I stifled them for myself as well. Mom knew my vulnerable side better than anyone, and I was afraid if I allowed my weakness and tears to break through with her, I would get lost in sorrow and never find my way out.

I actually got pretty good at feigning positive attitudes and spouting platitudes. But one evening, insult added to injury— literally—and pushed me over the edge, leaving my heart shattered into smithereens.

Mom arrived, and Phil prepared to leave when my mother-in-law showed up with the girls. They often met Daddy at the end of his shifts to visit for a while. This time out-of-town relatives accompanied them. I knew they were coming, but I wasn't prepared for the ensuing clamor. The small room quickly overflowed with people and chaotic conversation.

I enjoyed reconnecting with Phil's cousins, but I longed most of all to spend a few quality moments with my girls, who were now distracted by all the commotion. Each passing second, I knew the time of our dreaded separation drew closer.

"How about dinner at Timberline Steakhouse?" Phil suggested over the hubbub.

The group enthusiastically agreed, and I felt a fiery stab in my chest. My favorite restaurant! I looked at my husband in shock, but he didn't notice. How could the love of my life be so insensitive? I was invisible to this chatty, hungry bunch, my room merely a gathering place for their family reunion.

I waited for Phil's extended family to considerately give me a few minutes alone with him and the girls to say our good-byes. Nothing doing. The river of visitors that drifted through my doorway reversed its course and drifted out with a casual farewell, sweeping the girls away in their current. Phil lingered a moment longer, but dinner beckoned, and his empty stomach was like a hook pulling him out the door. Not knowing where to begin and not wanting to ruin his evening, I said nothing.

He kissed me and left. I was crushed. I felt betrayed. I wanted to cry out to God, but the heaviness was so sickening, I couldn't think. I couldn't find words that even began to describe the pain, the loneliness, and the despair. All I could do was hurt . . . and sob.

I could tell Mom wanted to cradle me in her arms as she watched me. I let it all go, diving headlong into the pit of sorrow. Mom instinctively held my hand and stroked my hair, knowing I wasn't just upset about dinner. This one night, added to all the others, seemed to carry a life sentence. A permanent decree that I would forever be

God Is Merciful

confined—held back, left out of my own life. It was an unfair verdict and one I could do nothing about.

"My entire world just walked out that door," I wailed.

Not knowing where to begin and not wanting to ruin his evening, I said nothing.

In the midst of my breakdown, the phone rang. My sister, Cynthia, told Mom that she and her family would be there in about thirty minutes. Her husband, Don, had some questions for me . . . about my faith. When Mom hung up the phone, she reluctantly told me they were coming. I couldn't believe it.

"Great," I said sarcastically, "perfect timing."

Through the years my sister seemed to have a knack for showing up at the wrong time. I wanted to see her—just not like this, not tonight. I prayed for composure and did my best to put on a happy face.

When they walked through the door, Mom took my nephew, Matt, outside to walk through the hospital's flower garden. Cynthia and Don pulled chairs close to my bed, wanting to know all the latest news from rehab.

As soon as the chitchat died down, Don started to explain what he had really come to ask. He had sensed peace in our family after my oldest sister's death from cancer three years before, and right on the heels of her passing, he saw that peace again after her son's tragic demise in a car accident. Now Don said he witnessed the same cool assurance . . . in me.

"I don't understand it," he said. "How can you be so calm when your world fell apart?"

"Ha!" I blurted.

The irony was dumbfounding. During one of my lowest moments

since the accident, Don asked about *peace*. I had to fess up. I couldn't fill him with a line of baloney and ignore the truth, especially considering how I had been anything but calm, cool, and collected a few moments earlier. Besides, I didn't have the strength or desire to build a facade.

"Things aren't always what they seem," I said. "Truth be known, I ache inside. I hate what happened to me."

Don was confused. I paused for a few seconds to think and then took a stab at what I thought he saw.

"Who God is to me has not changed because my body doesn't work or because I don't like the situation," I said, carefully choosing my words. "I can't turn away from God because my life hasn't worked out as I planned. God has always been there for me, and He's the only one who can help me now, so why would I shun Him?"

Don listened intently as I recapped how my relationship with God began. I was raised in the Lutheran church, and the pastor had read Matthew 6:33 as I knelt at the altar to accept Christ, "Seek the Kingdom of God above all else, and live righteously, and he will give you everything you need."

"God impressed upon me that this verse was truth I needed to heed closely," I said. "When I first heard it, I thought maybe God would make me rich if I followed Him." I laughed. "Okay, so maybe material wealth wasn't exactly what He had in mind. But as an adult, I've grown to understand that God knows my needs and will provide for them. As long as I keep Him first in my life, I don't need to worry. He'll take care of me."

Don looked bewildered.

"Maybe that sounds a bit unrealistic," I said, "but God has proven it. No one can argue God's provision when they look at me. Honestly, how many people survive flipping over on the highway at seventy miles an hour? And not only that, what are the chances that a nurse, respiratory therapist, and anesthesiologist would just happen to be

God Is Merciful

passing by the scene and stop to help? There is no such thing as coincidence, I'm convinced."

Cynthia nodded as I continued to illustrate God's hand in my life. Three months before the accident, my employer downsized, and my family was suddenly without health insurance. We took out personal health-insurance policies for each of us but never heard a word from the company. Two days after the wreck, our insurance cards arrived in the mail, showing coverage had started two weeks earlier. We then discovered the new company had *no limitation* on physical therapy! As an employee in the insurance industry, Don marveled.

"*That's* a miracle," he said.

"Yes, it is," I said. "God is working around us all the time. For example . . . "

I related that a couple of years before, Phil and I were looking for a used, full-sized, eight-cylinder conversion van to replace our minivan. Without telling anyone the amount we needed, we received a donation to cover it, to the penny. We got just what we were looking for—low mileage, beautiful comfort, a powerful engine—and we didn't spend a cent.

"Unfortunately, that blessing is now in the junkyard, but you won't believe the check we just got! God took care of us again."

A couple saw the story of our accident in an area newspaper. They, too, had been involved in an accident and recently received a settlement that exceeded what was necessary to replace their vehicle. So they sent the overage to us. The amount matched almost exactly what we lacked to replace our van with a brand-new model, wheelchair-lift equipped.

My audience was engrossed. Each story spurred another, building a case for God's indisputable presence and timely provision through Scripture, prayer, friends, and Sunday-morning sermons.

"I've learned Matthew 6:33 first hand," I said, "and my definition of

His provision has broadened dramatically. True wealth lies in the love of family and friends—and, of course, that of my heavenly Father.

"You know, brushes with tragedy always make what really matters in life perfectly clear. I may not like every turn of events, but I know my heavenly Father loves me. He's in charge, and that's all I need to know."

Suddenly I realized something. Cynthia and Don intended their visit for their benefit, but it was also for mine. I needed to see that the hard realities of the past two months paled in comparison with the unchanging power and love of my provider, comforter, encourager, and confidante . . . my very best friend.

As I rehearsed my history with God, a surprising surge of strength, certainty, joy, and, yes, even peace completely eradicated the stronghold of despair that clutched me only an hour earlier. My dear sister's infamous ability to call at the worst possible time was, as it turned out, perfect timing indeed. God's perfect timing.

God Is Merciful

God Is Father

A BURNING-BUSH SIGN

Mandy Foster, as told to Lisa Plowman Dolensky

"*W*hy can't we have one of those?" I'd turned and asked Tim, my husband of twelve years.

Flickering TV-screen light blued our faces and matched my mood. My desire was lit. But not because I wanted the latest advertised car or gizmo. My eyes were mesmerized by the news broadcast of orphaned children who'd survived Indonesia's then recent 2004 tsunami disaster.

Overwhelmed, longing washed over both of us. Our hearts were struck by images of needy children's faces. Our hopes were buoyant.

Tim's answer came to the rescue without hesitation, "Mandy, I'm ready!"

He and I'd been survivors in our own way. We were childless parents emerging from a most incredible spiritual storm. First, we were submerged in the depths of infertility. Then we were knocked down by the unexpected force of parental grief. We'd given up on having a child of our own when we finally became parents-to-be after ten and a half years of marriage, only to lose our baby during the first trimester when I miscarried.

We spent the next year exploring more heavy-duty fertility options in case something had changed, but nothing had. It was confirmed; we'd tried everything.

I couldn't help but wonder, *Where's God? Why did He allow me to get pregnant if I was going to lose this baby?*

I don't believe He caused my miscarriage. It was, however, part of God's plan and the kick in the pants we needed to get the ball rolling for us to adopt. Or maybe it was more like that first kick a mom feels when she's "with child." She might ask herself, "Did I just feel what I thought I felt?"

God's unconditional love was growing inside both Tim and me and preparing our hearts to want what He wanted for us. So I guess you could say we were sort of pregnant with God's preconceived plans, "expecting" to trust. Soon, we were cruising the Internet. A gazillion adoption services introduced us to the intrigue of international adoption. For us, it seemed like a more secure avenue for getting a child, as well as a faster process.

We wanted as young a child as possible, so he or she could grow up with us. We narrowed our search down to the two main countries were coming from: China and Guatemala. *But which one?*

One Saturday night Tim said, "Look, we know this is what the Lord plans for us. We don't doubt that. Let's pray for a burning-bush sign to tell us if we need to go to China or Guatemala.

Monday, I attended our monthly mission meeting. I came home and asked Tim, "Do you think it's kind of funny that three different ladies asked for prayers for three separate people on mission trips in Guatemala? No other countries were mentioned." He just laughed.

Tuesday, Tim was listening to the radio and heard an announcer, "Come see U.S. vs. Guatemala in World Cup Soccer, first time ever played in Birmingham."

Wednesday, a travel magazine arrived in our mailbox—the cover story on Antiqua, Guatemala's oldest city.

We discussed, "Are we being Guatemala sensitive? Are we hearing

God Is Father

anything about China or anyplace else?" So we decided to listen for China and be more perceptive about other places.

But Thursday, Tim heard on the radio that the U.S. secretary of defense would be touring Guatemala.

Friday, we compared notes. Nothing else happened. We continued to pray and keep the adoption desires of our hearts secret.

Saturday, some of my father's visiting senior-citizen cousins met us for dinner. Tim asked, "Have y'all taken any exciting trips lately?"

> "I don't know if it's a burning bush,
> but I certainly smell smoke."

"We just went to Honduras," they replied.

"How long did you stay in Honduras?" asked Tim.

"Actually, we only spent one day in Honduras, but we spent ten days in Guatemala."

I squeezed Tim's leg under the table. You would've thought I'd just dilated ten centimeters. I *could feel in my gut and see what was ahead— God willing, one way or another we were having a baby!*

Driving home I cross-examined, "Tim, do you think we're getting a burning-bush sign?"

"Mandy, I don't know if it's a burning bush, but I certainly smell smoke."

Days passed. Wednesday, after church Tim relaxed watching television while I paced.

"Mandy, what's wrong with you?"

I stopped right in front of the television. I snapped, "Nothing's wrong! Are we doing this adoption?"

"Yes, we've already decided that."

I demanded, "Well, which country? Which agency?"

"Hon, we prayed for a burning-bush sign, and I think God's telling us Guatemala."

"Tim, how can we really be sure? What country is it?"

"Guatemala!" shouted the TV actor as he talked on his cell phone.

"Tim, what'd he just say?"

Before Tim could answer, an actress screamed on the episode, "It's Guatemala!"

Chills ran down my spine.

I needed a sanity check. "Tim, can God talk to you through the television?"

"He just did!"

We slept great that night, perhaps because we were assured of God's message . . . or because He'd hit us over the head so many times with it.

The next day I contacted the first agency on my short list and told them, "We're really interested in Guatemala adoptions." They automatically discouraged Guatemala, which let me know we didn't want to use them.

Spring break thankfully provided an escape, and at the last minute our plans to go to Tennessee were changed to go to southern Alabama.

On our second day there we headed out for a restaurant, not even thinking about adoption.

"Ugh!" Tim groaned. "I missed the road to downtown, but if I keep going, surely there'll be a road that leads into it."

Suddenly, the car in front of us stopped at a green light.

Tim braked muttering, "What are they doing?"

Then we realized it had stopped to give a flashing police car clearance at the intersection. While the traffic light changed from yellow to red, my eyes—which normally can't see ten feet in front of me—spotted a business sign about a block ahead: Children of the World International Adoption Agency.

God Is Father

"Tim, that's the adoption agency that's having a meeting near us next month."

"Let's go talk to them," Tim volunteered.

Soon we were in the agency foyer.

A man greeted us, and we expressed our interest in adopting from Guatemala. The woman who founded the agency and her daughter, who handled Guatemala adoptions spoke with us. They asked, "How did you find us?"

As I explained, the founder's stare and words penetrated my soul, "God sent you here today. Don't you know that?"

We spent hours talking, and before we departed, the founder encouraged us to pray about it. She gave us pamphlets, her blessing, and recommendations for taking a leap of faith.

We left and drove about five miles down the road before picking up the cell phone. "Can we come back tomorrow?" we asked.

Next we stopped at the bookstore. The cashier and a customer were talking. We couldn't help overhearing, "My girlfriend's on a mission trip in Central America," the customer said.

Tim cocked his head and confidently whispered, "Mandy, just watch this."

Tim cut his eyes at me as he asked the young man, "Where in Central America?"

"Guatemala."

Now we were sure that our baby was in Guatemala.

The next morning we were ready to tell the agency to begin processing the papers. Tim was too nervous to eat much. *Morning sickness?* He grabbed a banana. His eyes zoomed in on the Chiquita label. "Look! It's made in Guatemala!"

The next thing we knew, we were getting the baby's room ready, and I was cleaning out my supplies from teaching elementary school. As I started to discard a puppet, Tim walked in and said, "Don't get rid of this one. José will like it!"

"José?" I asked. "No way."

"Oh, Mandy, that's just a nickname for the baby. It's a common Hispanic name."

"José? Okay!"

As we waited through the months, we relentlessly pursued paper work, biographies, physicals, reference letters, finance reports, background checks, social-worker home studies, etc. Each phase intensified like contractions.

Exhale. The labor finally paid off. The agency referral call came after nine months.

"Are you sitting down?" the woman asked when Tim answered the phone. "We have a baby boy for you, and his name is José." She continued, "We handle about forty Guatemalan adoptions a year, and haven't had a José in six years."

We were floored by God's sense of humor. We decided to rename our child Seth, which means, "God's chosen one."

Six months later we arrived in Guatemala to claim him. Once on the plane back to the States, our tensions released and prayers calmed my nerves during turbulence. A Guatemalan man with a work visa sat beside Tim and started talking to him. His name? José.

For me, it was just another reminder of God's presence. I knew He would be with us always.

God Is Father

God Is Rescuer

THE DRAGON SLAYER

David Evans, as told to Karen Evans

I'm late! I thought, glancing at my watch.

My wife and daughter expected me at the ballpark. But at the last minute I decided to dash by our apartment first. We were house-sitting for some friends, and I'd forgotten to take my guitar to their home. I wanted to get it for praise practice at church that night and didn't want to go back home after the game.

It won't hurt if I'm just a few more minutes late, I thought. I grabbed my guitar and then took another few minutes to call my dad before heading out.

An acrid odor seeped into the apartment. "Dad, I've got to go, I think I smell smoke!" I abruptly hung up and shoved the cell phone into my pocket. Dropping my guitar on the couch, I scanned the apartment. Nothing seemed wrong.

I jerked open the front door and followed the burning smell down the hallway. Dashing to my neighbor's apartment, I saw gray mushrooms of smoke emerging through their open door.

"Hey, anybody in here?" I yelled. A wall of acrid smoke assaulted my eyes and choked my breath as I looked in. I touched the doorknob. It was still cool, so I cautiously stepped inside. I couldn't see but knew the layout was the same as our apartment's.

"Hello, anyone here?" I shouted again, hitting my shin on something. *I'd better feel my way around the furniture as I search.*

"In here . . . I'm in here," a man's voice yelled. Following the voice, I found my neighbor dazed and disoriented. He paced, shaking his head in disbelief as if trying to wake from a bad dream.

"Hey, what's going on?" I asked. My words broke up as the smoke closed my throat.

"I don't know! I just got here. My son must have just left," he sputtered, raising his hands to cover his mouth.

In the kitchen an explosion of bright orange flames whooshed and crackled through the dense smoke, leaping violently and licking the cabinets and oven like the spitfire of an angry dragon. In the light of the fire we saw a blackened mass of something on the stove.

I wrestled the phone from my pocket and called 911. The operator asked for our location and information. She told us to stay on the line while the firemen were contacted.

Meanwhile, we ran to the bathroom and snatched towels. After dousing them with water from the tub and sink, we wrapped them around our noses and mouths to keep the strangling smoke at bay.

The 911 operator tried to give us calm instructions, but the fire bellowed and hissed in our ears, deafening her words. I never knew fire was so loud. As I answered her questions, I breathed in great amounts of the noxious smoke.

> The fire bellowed and hissed in our ears, deafening the operator's words.

Arms cradling more drenched towels, we ran to the kitchen. We then began our game of Whack-a-Mole with the dragon. The black unidentifiable mass on the stove jumped up and down in the air and crumbled with each frantic whack. The hungry flames chomped at the oven vent, determined to burn and conquer anything in their way. Our towels became swords and shields. Every couple of seconds we

God Is Rescuer

stopped to rewet them as the intense heat dried them out. We became absolutely maniacal with our whacking.

Somewhere in time we heard quiet instead of crackle and saw gray air instead of neon orange. Straining through the smoke, we saw we had defeated the flames. Breathless from exertion and smoke inhalation and confident our expert fire demolition was complete, we unwound our mummylike wraps from our hands and face. The lingering smoke and stench practically gagged me.

I heard a voice coming from my pants pocket. *Oh, the 911 operator, I forgot I was still on the line.*

I explained how our heroic and valiant efforts saved the day and we had extinguished the fire. "Ha, you can call us the dragon slayers!"

She grudgingly acknowledged our conquest and canceled the call for the firemen. We breathed a sigh of relief as we realized that because our apartments are on the second floor, the firemen would have had to use their water hose, which would have made a bigger mess for everyone.

I wiped my forehead with the crook of my arm. We blinked our swollen, bloodshot eyes, trying to clear out the smoke and soot. As we coughed, little sooty puff clouds danced around our heads. We groped our way outside for some fresh air, but I still smelled smoke. The world behaving normally outside clashed with what had just happened inside. Gratefully, we took deep breaths of clean air.

I realized my dad did not know what was going on. I flipped open my phone and called him, my fingers leaving black marks on each number I punched. I knew he would be praying and concerned since I had hung up on him so suddenly.

"Dad, we're okay! My neighbor's kitchen was on fire. It's totally ruined," I reported, walking back to my apartment. "My apartment smells, but we'll just need to air it out." I explained how it was really nothing, still pumped from the experience.

When I hung up the phone, my adrenalin plunged, and I dropped into a chair, worn out by the enormity of it all. I sat astounded to think about what just occurred. What if my neighbor and I had not both come home at the same time? What damage might have been done? My knees became a little weak and my head dizzy. As I took a minute to thank the One who watched over me, my heart filled with gratitude. I knew God directed my steps to make this last-minute stop at the apartment instead of going straight to the game. Otherwise, since we weren't even staying at the apartment, I wouldn't have been there to help my neighbor. And I honestly doubted that he could have handled the fire alone.

I eventually made it to the softball game. I was very late, of course, but I had a good excuse. I wore the same ash- and soot-covered clothes as proof and, of course, to impress my daughter, which it did.

As I watched my daughter play, I contemplated the experience. I just "happened" to go by the apartment to get my guitar before the softball game and just "happened" to stay a little longer to call my dad. My neighbor just "happened" to come home at the right time, too. Coincidence? No, God had guided my steps. Thank you, Lord.

God Is Pure

TWICE-FOUND TREASURE

Elisa Yager

I was proud of my accomplishment; my daughter Beth had become a bargain hunter at the age of ten. I was not nearly her age when the flea-market bug bit me, much to my mother's chagrin. Now, three years into her practical education, we zipped up our jackets to ward off the chill permeating the spring morning.

With our lists in hand, Beth and I dove into the sea of flea-market vendors to find buried treasures.

My list was brief—anything antique would satisfy. But the practical side of me also reminded me to look for utilitarian finds: glass bowls, my favorite Homer Laughlin dishes, and anything to make my home feel more welcoming to friends and family.

Beth's list was more specific: bling, flashy jewelry, glitter nail polish, castoff handbags in good condition, and baskets to organize the plethora of makeup and jewelry stashed in her dresser drawers. If she happened to find a teddy bear that inaudibly said, "Take me home," that would also be a great find.

We passed vendors selling the entire contents of their homes. Others sold plants in anticipation of Mother's Day just around the corner. A local scouting troop was selling a hodgepodge of items.

I found an occasional antique and conferred with Beth. "Should I buy it?" "Is it too expensive?" "Do I need it?" "Where could I put it?"

Little by little our canvas bags became heavier and our wallets lighter. We were having a great day.

As we approached the last row of tables, Beth suggested we skip them and head home. But I was not to be deterred from digging for more treasure. I asked for a few more tables, and Beth agreed hesitantly. We scooted to the table where a man dug through a stack of antique books. Beth saw the glimmer in my eyes and knew it could be a long "few more tables."

"C'mon, Mom, I'm tired. Let's go home," Beth complained.

"I'm almost done," I replied as I examined the book in my hand. I picked up other books, flipped a few pages, and put them down again.

Then a small, thick book caught my attention, and I grabbed it seconds before the man next to me got his large hand on it. I peered at the spine: *Holy Bible*. Time and handling had worn away the gold leaf, but the engraved letters on the spine were unmistakable.

"Mom, c'mon. I have to sit down. My feet are killing me!"

"Beth, look. It's a Bible."

"You don't need any more Bibles. You have enough to supply an entire congregation. Besides, the cover is dirty and it smells."

"The binding is in good condition, and I've never seen a Bible so small." I turned to the first page and found a copyright date of 1854. I flipped through the pages quickly to make sure none were torn. I held it up and asked the elderly vendor the price. He took it from my hand and examined it.

Lord, let it be a reasonable price. You know I don't have much money left.

"Oh, let's see . . . how about . . . mmmm . . . a dollar fifty?"

"Mom, it's not worth ten cents. It smells and it's dirty."

"I really like this little Bible. I'm going to take it."

I paid, wrapped it in some excess newspaper I found in my bag,

God Is Pure

and quickly stashed the Bible away as Beth and I headed toward the car. The ride home was quiet. Beth dozed as I thought about the wonderful treasures I had found that morning.

Our purchases unloaded in the kitchen, I turned my attention to my last purchase of the day. Sitting on the couch, I carefully turned the old, fragile pages. I noticed that one of the front pages had faint writing—an inscription I had not seen earlier. The writing had faded, but I was able to read, *Presented to Adela Whittesey from her owner, ending her slavery, January 1861.*

Tears filled my eyes, as reality hit deep in my heart, and American history became alive.

> ## Presented to Adela Whittesey from her owner, ending her slavery, January 1861.

I'd later learn that I had purchased a pocket Bible typical of those carried into battle by Civil War soldiers. I wondered who originally owned the Bible and had given it to Adela Whittesey along with her freedom.

Not only did the Bible document the historical act of physical freedom for one particular American, but it also provided spiritual freedom. I flipped through the worn pages. Scriptures were underlined. It was evident that the owners of this little Bible used it often.

Later that afternoon when Beth returned from visiting a friend, I showed her the inscription. She was overwhelmed by the fact that the little Bible once belonged to a former slave and couldn't wait to tell her history class what "we" had found at the flea market, since the class was studying the Civil War and Reconstruction. The timing couldn't have been better.

Later that evening before she went to bed, Beth knocked on my bedroom door. She sat on my bed with a sheepish look on her face.

"I'm sorry for trying to talk you out of buying that Bible. If I had known what was written in it, I would never have said anything."

Not missing the opportunity to teach a precious life lesson, I used the flea market as an example for her.

"Treasures can be easy to find or they can take a little digging. Sometimes, like today, you can find a treasure and not even know it right away. That Bible was old, and, yes, it smelled musty, but Adela found a treasure in that Bible, and you and I found a treasure inside it too, many years after Adela found hers."

"Thanks, Mom," Beth replied.

"Thanks? For what?"

"For reminding me not to judge a book by its cover . . . or its smell. Next time I'll look inside first." She gave me a hug and left. I bowed my head and thanked God for the gift of my daughter and for teaching us both about treasures often hidden where we least expect to find them.

God Is Pure

God Is Deliverer

NEVER-ENDING LOVE

Linda Holloway

"*A*re you in trouble? My dream about you scared me," said a familiar voice from my childhood and teen years. Sam McBee had tracked me down through my parents. We hadn't seen each other for at least five or six years.

"Trouble? No, I'm not in trouble. I'm okay."

My parents had shocked me the night before when they phoned to tell me Sam had contacted them. He didn't live far from their suburban Chicago home.

"Sam remembered that we had moved up here with my job after you graduated from high school. He found our number in the phone book," Daddy said.

I asked if Sam knew I'd gotten divorced after an unhappy two-year marriage.

"Oh, he knew you married and left Georgia, but he didn't know about the divorce. He seemed anxious to talk with you."

I wrote down Sam's number and agreed to call him the next evening.

After Sam answered the phone when I called him, his question caught me off guard. *What a strange question. Am I in trouble? Why would Sam ask such a thing?*

"Linda, I dreamed about you last week. Your face looked drawn, and your eyes stared vacantly here and there. You stood alone, and a black mist closed in around you. Fear gripped me as you disappeared in the dark. I woke up screaming your name."

"What a weird dream!"

Sam cleared his throat. "I sensed you were in trouble and needed help right away, so I started looking for you. Now I feel a little silly."

> "I sensed you were in trouble and needed help right away, so I started looking for you."

A battle between truth and a lie raged inside me. My lifestyle in the two years since the divorce reflected our worldly culture, not Jesus. I wasn't the girl Sam had known in church.

"Well, Sam, I appreciate your calling. I'm coming to Chicago for Christmas. Maybe we could get together."

"Really? I'd like to see you. You must think I'm crazy."

"No. Just a concerned old friend. There might be a little truth to your dream. We'll talk when I get there."

After my divorce I felt free—free from lies, emotional abuse, and pain. My ex-husband, a preacher's kid, had not treated me like he'd been taught to treat a wife. Both of us grew up in church, but the only time we entered one was to marry. We were young and could hardly wait to shake off the restraints of Christian families. The misery of that marriage drove me to consider suicide as a pathway to peace, but divorce remedied the problem. Or so I thought.

Sam's call focused my attention on the emptiness of my life. *I know I shouldn't go to the clubs. I feel almost dirty when I get home. I've dated bunches of guys—mostly losers. What should I expect at a bar? Sam's dream could be right. I do feel like I'm in a dark pit at times.*

The plane ride to Chicago from my home in Kansas City was

God Is Deliverer

uneventful until we approached O'Hare. As we circled the airport again and again, I mulled over my conversation with Sam. I wondered what he looked like and if he'd ever married. He didn't mention a wife or family when we talked.

What will I tell him? It could be embarrassing. Oh, I probably shouldn't tell him anything. We'll just chat and reminisce and then go back to our respective lives.

Mama met me at the baggage carousel. She rushed at a big man who pushed me aside to get his suitcase. He retreated from the angry white-haired little lady.

"Welcome to Chicago, huh?" I said.

What would Mama think if she knew my behavior at home? She's proud that I'm a teacher, but what would she say about the bars and the men?

I shook off the troubling thoughts and walked out to see Daddy. We chatted during the ride to their apartment.

"Well, are you going to see Sam while you're here?" Mama waited at least five minutes before she asked.

We acted like two shy adolescents for the first few minutes.

"I think so. I'll call him tonight, and we'll set a time and place."

"You know he must really want to see you to go to such effort to find you. He even thought you were still married but got in touch with us anyway," Daddy said. "Sam was a nice boy. Did you ever date?"

"Oh, no. Sam was too tame for me."

I called Sam after supper, and we agreed to meet for lunch two days later. The opportunity to see someone from happier days excited me. On the other hand, it also made me nervous.

Sam's directions to the restaurant were simple, and I arrived ten minutes early. When I entered, a tall man stood and waved. I easily recognized Sam and joined him. He surprised me with a quick hug before we sat.

We acted like two shy adolescents for the first few minutes. However, after we ordered, we slipped into easy, comfortable conversation. Sam showed authentic concern for me, and I soon spilled my story to him.

"Sam, your dream about me was true. I know I shouldn't be living the way I do. It's wrong."

Sam listened to my story with patience. If he felt disappointment or disgust, he didn't show it.

"Linda, I believe God sent the dream to get your attention. He's never quit loving you."

"Maybe. He's tried to get my attention before, but I tuned Him out. I guess He knew you would persist until you found me. You're probably the only one from our old church who lives near my parents or me. He knew who to send and who would come. Thank you."

After our two-hour lunch, I drove back to my parents' home. Sweet warmth flowed through me.

"Father God, thank you for still loving me. And thank *you* for Sam."

Our conversation replayed in my mind throughout the rest of my visit. I didn't tell my parents the whole story. In fact, I didn't tell them much at all. I only related the part about the dream and Sam's belief that God sent it.

"God loves me even if I haven't been to church in a few years," I said.

I let them draw their own conclusions, aware that I purposefully misled them. My action was another clue as to how far down the wrong road I'd traveled.

God Is Deliverer

When I returned to my apartment, I dug out my Bible from the box of books I'd never unpacked. Its white leather cover reminded me of my childhood. The sweet, familiar song "Jesus Loves Me" formed on my lips and brought tears to my eyes.

I'd like to say that my life changed dramatically after my Chicago trip. However, change happened slowly. It took time to break free from the lifestyle I had fallen into while I had searched for love and approval.

Sam and I lost contact, but that special lunch of over thirty years ago etched itself in my memory. God's extravagant display of love still takes my breath away and swells my heart with delight and gratitude.

God Is Light

Little Points of Light

Dianne E. Butts

*T*hat sunny June Saturday I finally had energy to do some things I enjoyed. I planted pink dianthus in the gardens on the south side of the house we'd purchased a year earlier. For years to come, they would produce mounds of pink flowers along the path separating the two gardens. I planted a pink rose. A label on the pot promised that the vendor would send part of my purchase price to breast cancer research. I planted reblooming daylilies and ground cover to fill in between the plants. I ran drip lines so all these flowers would survive our hot summer months without depending on me to have energy to water them daily.

The noonday sun grew hotter. I tugged off my gloves and tossed them into my garden tote. My legs felt weak as I gathered my tools and emptied flowerpots. I trudged up the slope to the garage where my husband, Hal, tinkered.

After we went inside and had a glass of iced tea, I felt reenergized enough to conquer the next project on my to-do list. I sell a line of biker pins—those pins motorcyclists like to wear on their vests that say things like "Jesus Saves Bikers Too" and "Jesus Happens." I had an order to fill and ship before the post office closed that afternoon. I pulled out my box of biker pins and packaged the order for mailing. I returned the inventory to the box and replaced it in my office closet. Gathering my purse and keys, I headed out through the garage.

"I'll be back," I told Hal. I rolled down the window and hung my arm out to soak up the pleasant June sun as I drove to the post office.

After standing in line to mail the package, I climbed into the car feeling weariness overwhelm me. Time to go home, turn on the television, curl up on the couch, and rest. I turned out of the post office parking lot onto the busy street.

That's when I saw it.

The prongs that held the diamond in my beautiful gold wedding ring stood empty, reaching, grasping after something they no longer held.

"Oh," I said out loud. "My diamond's gone!"

My stomach turned. I'd been planning to get the prongs checked. Why hadn't I made the time to get it done—even with everything else going on?

The prongs that held the diamond in my beautiful gold wedding ring stood empty, reaching, grasping after something they no longer held.

"Oh, Lord," I prayed, "will You please help me find my diamond?"

There was no place to pull over. I drove, scanning the roadway for any little point of light.

When had I last seen it? Was it there this morning? Had it fallen out in the garden, buried with one of those plants? Maybe it was in the house. Had it fallen into the carpet?

Oh, and there was that box of biker pins. I could look to see if it had fallen in there.

But what if I had lost the diamond as my hand dangled out the window on the way to the post office? What were the chances of finding it—no matter where I'd lost it?

I pulled into the driveway, and Hal came to greet me. As I stepped out of the car, the tears came. "I lost my diamond!" I cried, holding my left hand out for him to see.

"Oh no!" he said, clearly sharing my pain.

"Maybe it's in my garden glove," I said, heading for the tote.

"I'll help you look," he said. He began to scan the garage floor. I carefully checked the ring finger in my left glove, feeling for a diamond-sized rock, turning it inside out and checking each finger. Hal walked to the garden, surveying the gravel pathway along the way. I joined him, searching the ground around the newly planted flowers.

Lord, I prayed again, *will You please help me find my diamond?*

Doubt felt like a hard lump of coal in my stomach. What were the chances of finding a tiny diamond in a garden or in a house or along a city street?

I fought off the discouraging thoughts trying to push their way into my mind, but I was losing that battle. We'd been through so much the last six months. Hadn't we suffered enough?

It was January when I got the phone call every woman dreads. "Dianne, we see something on your mammogram." Little points of light on the X-ray indicated "calcifications," which could indicate cancer. Doctors sent me for a needle biopsy in February. In March I got the diagnosis: it was cancer.

On the last day of March, doctors performed a mastectomy—only twelve days before our twenty-fifth anniversary.

We had talked about doing something special for our twenty-fifth—maybe a fancy trip. Instead I was forced to stay at home, recovering from surgery. I'd opted for reconstruction, so three more surgeries lay ahead. We joked that instead of a trip, we'd be getting a partially new body for our twenty-fifth. But more seriously, we knew the mastectomy had given us back my life.

God Is Light

I tried to tell myself it was only a diamond. We had the more important thing: a good marriage. The diamond and the ring that was supposed to hold it were only a symbol. We had our lives.

Weariness covered me like a blanket.

"We'll get another one," Hal said. I hugged him. I loved his generous heart, his willingness to always try to make things right. But my heart still broke with the loss of the diamond he had placed on my finger twenty-five years earlier.

I drove back to the post office, hoping to see a little point of sunlight reflect off the gem. I remembered again to search the pin box at home in the closet. *Don't forget,* I thought. I searched the post-office lobby and the ground where I had parked earlier. Nothing.

Back home, Hal was on his hands and knees searching the living room carpet. Back in the garage, I ran my hands over the carpeted floor of the car.

I wasn't the only one who had lost a diamond. My friend Gayle had not realized her wedding ring had slipped off as she raked leaves and loaded them into the back of a pickup. Like me, she was horrified to discover it gone, and like me, she had desperately prayed, asking God to help her find it. After searching and searching, in the sunlight Gayle had seen a sparkle among the leaves and followed it to her ring lying in the bed of the pickup.

I fought the thought pushing into my mind. *God does those things for other people, but that's no guarantee He'll do the same for me.*

When my friend, Jennie, lost the diamond out of her wedding ring, I blurted out: "I have this feeling you'll find it." Weeks later Jennie found the loose diamond on top of a support board between the slats of their second-story deck. I said, "I knew you'd find it."

What I'd give to get one of those feelings now about my own diamond. But I felt only exhausted and defeated.

He doesn't do things like that for me.

I scolded myself for allowing that thought to enter my mind. I refused to feel sorry for myself.

I trudged in from the garage. Hal had searched the whole house with no luck. I tried to think of where else I had been that day.

Tired as I was, it was time to start dinner. I headed to the kitchen.

Look inside the box. That thought whispered to my mind again.

Oh yeah. I'd forgotten again. I went to the closet, pulled out the box, and unloaded its contents. Nothing. I peered into the dark bottom of the narrow box. It looked clean and empty. I tilted the box and watched a miniature dust bunny rattle across the bottom from one corner to the other.

Well, I had tried. I'd looked everywhere I could think of.

I replaced the biker pins back in the box. I was closing the top when it occurred to me: *dust doesn't rattle.*

I flipped open the box and unloaded it for the third time that day. Looking down at the bottom of the empty box, I tilted it. Again, that little ball of dust tumbled and rattled from corner to corner.

I reached down into the corner of the box and gingerly grabbed it. I felt a hard core inside the ball of dust. I placed the little ball in the palm of my hand and blew the dust away. Sitting in my palm was the brightest, most sparkly diamond I'd ever seen. I'd never seen my diamond outside its setting. I was astounded at its fire, its points of light reflecting colors in glints of blue and yellow and glowing bright white.

Hal came in looking for me. Did I want to get take-out for dinner?

"I found it!" I said, holding the sparkling points of light up for him to see. "Thank you, Lord!" I said out loud.

We wrapped the diamond in a tissue and tucked it into an envelope

God Is Light

with my ring. We'd take it to a jeweler another day. For now, I just felt like I would burst with joy.

Thank you, God, I said silently over and over.

Little points of light. He had shown me where to find my diamond.

Little points of light had alerted doctors to my cancer early so I had an excellent chance to recover.

God loved me every bit as much as He loved Gayle and Jennie. He was taking care of me—He had restored both my diamond and my health.

God Is Eternal

THE ULTIMATE EYE-OPENING EXPERIENCE

Donald E. Phillips

As a hospice chaplain, I've seen many people die. For eight years my daily work has been to connect with dying patients and their families and friends, to support those who serve them, and to educate and encourage others with memorial services, grief counseling, and support of pastors and parishioners.

While many people fear or shun encounters related to those who are actively dying, I have discovered that we can learn much from them.

One of the most memorable, eye-opening experiences of my life occurred as I journeyed with my friend Dale and his dedicated wife, Sara, who were both in their nineties when I knew them as a hospice chaplain. I first visited them when they lived in an apartment, convenient for their later years.

We had many good visits. I was so comfortable visiting the couple that once I even momentarily fell asleep while talking with Dale. That was a bit embarrassing since he had to wake me up. They became like family as we shared past and present experiences.

Dale and Sara were solid Christians, and Dale had been chairman of the board at his local church and a community leader. We reminisced about his wartime experiences, his factory work in Cannery Row in California, his grocery store work in Wichita,

Kansas, and the small Kansas town where he now lived and had owned a grocery store.

One dramatic event occurred while Dale and Sara were still in their apartment. One mealtime Dale seriously choked on a piece of chicken and appeared to be in danger of dying. But it wasn't quite his time yet.

Sara, about ninety, was much smaller than Dale and did most of her getting around with a walker. But she had the courage, insight, and determination—and likely divine empowerment—to grab Dale, use the Heimlich maneuver, and save his life by dislodging the food that was choking him.

Eventually Dale and Sara reluctantly decided it was a bit too hard for them to keep the apartment, so they moved to an assisted-living facility in a nearby town.

Their quarters were pleasant. We continued sharing happily and enjoyed, as always during our visits, times of prayer.

Gradually Dale's physical condition, affected by a type of cancer, caused him to decline more. He had to transfer to a skilled-nursing facility nearby. I thought that might be the last stop for him, but he was resilient, even at ninety, and hung in there.

But he eventually declined again and had to be transferred to a large hospital in a nearby city. I had known him at his apartment, his assisted-living quarters, a nursing home, and now the hospital. In the hospital he sensed his time was getting shorter, but he was still positive, still upbeat.

After several days in the hospital, he was transferred yet again to the hospice's residential care center. I visited him there twice. The first time he was his old self, relaxed, peaceful, and very talkative. The second time, which was only a week later, he seemed unconscious. He did not respond when I spoke to him. Sara and the couple's daughter were in the room, so I sat to talk with them. I kept looking back at

Dale, lying flat on his back, motionless in bed. This went on for about twenty minutes.

Suddenly Dale stirred, and I stood to see if he was reviving. That's when I had the ultimate eye-opening experience. Dale, previously still, now rose from the waist—not grabbing at the edges and needing help, as he had before—with eyes wide open.

> I kept looking back at Dale,
> lying flat on his back, motionless in bed.

I was standing directly in front of him, and could see a tear in one eye. I do not think he was looking at me. I believe he was seeing something beyond this life. His gaze and attention were riveted.

What was it? What did he see? Why was there suddenly a tear in his eye? I believe he was seeing God or heavenly things. He was looking beyond this world into the next. I believe he was experiencing what was said of that great man of faith, Abraham, in Genesis 25:8, "He died at a ripe old age, having lived a long and satisfying life. He breathed his last and joined his ancestors in death."

While Dale sat up, he breathed in and out a couple of times. He then rested back on his bed, eyes closed, and breathed once or twice more. And then his breath ceased.

I believe he also experienced, not only physically but spiritually, the fulfillment the apostle Paul prayed for believers in Ephesians 1:18 when he wrote: "I pray that your hearts will be flooded with light so that you can understand the confident hope he has given to those he called—his holy people who are his rich and glorious inheritance."

That day, I believe I witnessed Dale's realization of those promises, physical and spiritual. I believe I watched a man who saw that God was with him as he finished his earthly journey.

God Is Eternal

In Dale's eyes, I believe I saw confirmation that what the Bible teaches is true. Psalm 116:15 tells us, "The LORD cares deeply when his loved ones die." As a chaplain, I have learned that God cares for us throughout our journey in this world . . . and that care will last all the days of our lives and beyond.

God Is Love

MANY GIFTS IN ONE

Lisa Plowman Dolensky

Will he laugh or squeal first? I wondered.

There's nothing quite like planning a surprise for your child. Even when you're a pregnant and weary waddler with an energetic toddler. I was barely able to put one swollen foot in front of the other as Max, my two-year-old son, dashed down the store's toy aisle, giggling all the way.

To any onlookers it probably appeared to be a comical race as both our bodies were belly-first propelled, with whizzing blurs of moving arms and legs following. I don't think I'd seen my own feet in months. It took every ounce of anticipation and adrenalin to keep up with Max. I ignored every kick and Braxton Hicks contraction and the bulge of my second pregnancy. I was feeling every bit of nine months, and my due date was less than two weeks away.

Thank goodness this is today's last stop.

I'd so looked forward to the toy-aisle visit. Instead of window-shopping as usual, Max would be getting a popping-balls push-toy vacuum like I had when I was a kid. It would be our first memory of purchasing a toy together.

On other visits Max had been allowed, with my careful supervision, to joyfully examine books, balls, plastic push mowers, and wooden toy trains. The store had an interactive and user-friendly atmosphere. Max had been blessed with a cooperative nature for the most part. Luckily, he'd always willingly put the toys back when told and never fussed to keep them. Or at least not much. I didn't think he understood yet that this store was a place where you could buy things to take home.

Today I was anxious to see his look of excitement when we officially walked out with a toy he could claim as his very own.

Max handled his favorite toys, and then I introduced him to the toy "vacuum."

"Vrrrooommm! Look at what Mommy's got for you!"

He squealed first, his little body trembling with delight. Then he began to push the vacuum with gusto. I beamed with pride because my newfound motherly instinct was right on target. He loved it. "Pop-pop-pop!"

For me the sound was pleasantly familiar. I convinced myself, *you can certainly tune that out.* No batteries required—just kid power.

I let Max roll and push it around for more than five minutes. Then I gently took it from his hands and began explaining, "Mommy's going to buy this for you. . . . "

But before I could finish my sentence, my darling's face fell, tears began gushing, and he opened his mouth wider than ever in a record-decibel piercing bawl! The resonation nearly threw me into labor.

He assumed I was routinely returning the toy to a shelf, and with full adhesive reflex he gripped the vacuum's handle with all his strength. Max held on with hands, legs, and feet. His all. Refusing to let go, he fell onto his back and nearly pulled this great mother load down with him.

He shrieked between sobs, "Mine! Mine!"

Where was the laughter?

My own mouth gaped open, but nothing came out. I was in shock and at a loss for words. *Had the terrible twos arrived this second? Just in time for baby?* Panicked, I looked around for any welcomed parental support.

I hoped to hear the manager's voice break in over the speaker's music, "Parent support needed aisle nine."

Instead, passersby either ignored us or threw us disgusted looks. I imagined words that went with their glances: *Spoiled brat. Some mother she is.*

> I hoped to hear the manager's voice break in over the speaker's music, "Parent support needed aisle nine."

My own motherly pride bubble burst as I felt inexperienced and unseasoned for this trying moment. Everything I'd been reading about effectively disciplining children was now forgotten. All I could lucidly think to do was pray silently, *Lord, please help me. What should I do?*

Heat rushed from my toes and blushed up to my face. I could feel the baby within knot and harden, as if in sympathetic tension. Max's little face scrunched and reddened. But for different reasons than mine.

My inner voice said, *Just let him cry it out, but don't give in. Hang tough.*

This was to be my first memorable declaration of tough love. I felt unsure as tears filled my eyes. The gift-giving fantasy was over. The next few seconds passed like an eternity. Max flailed his body until exhausted. Then he wept more softly, and in his weak moment I began to pry the handle from him. He screamed again. Then he balled his fists and punched the air. *Was this my child?*

I felt a stare and sheepishly looked around as I disappointedly placed the toy high out of reach. A wrinkled, gray-haired, hunched woman, who was probably in her seventies, stood there smiling and tapping her walking cane. We had her attention, and she suddenly had mine. She lifted the cane and pointed to Max, saying, "If he were just a little bit older, you could just leave'm here."

Her wit and wisdom made me laugh unexpectedly.

Then she said more affirming words: "Let him wear himself out, but don't let him get his way."

She hobbled over to a vacant shopping cart and pushed it up beside us. She helped coax him up, encouraged him to listen to me, and helped me lift him into the cart. Then she placed her cold hand on my shoulder and said words my tired heart needed so desperately to hear, "You're a good mother."

She placed her cold hand on my shoulder and said words my tired heart needed so desperately to hear, "You're a good mother."

I said, "Thanks for coming to the rescue. So how many children do you have?"

My kind stranger replied, "Five too many, but never enough."

She slowly walked away as I began to wipe Max's runny nose. When I looked up, she had rounded the corner, and I never saw her again.

Pooped and with spirits popped, I zigzagged down aisles until I could cart a slumping, half-dozing child out of the store. Tears slowly rolled down my own cheeks because I'd wanted this special gift to happen before the baby arrived. My husband often traveled out of town, my energy was getting low, and I knew we'd probably missed one of the best opportunities. It would just have to wait. There were more important things in life. I prayed, *God please forgive me for feeling sorry for myself.*

I waddled to my car, lifted Max's limber body into the car, and buckled him into his car seat. He now looked so angelic in slouched slumber. It began to mist rain. I locked the car.

I walked just a few steps to return the buggy to the designated shed. Just as I pushed it in, I noticed that the cart in front of it had a full shopping bag left in the tot-sit spot. I sighed reluctantly and grumbled, "Oh, great. Now I'll have to return this bag someone accidentally left, wake up Max, and carry him back in to do so."

I reached for the bag. I noticed a familiar blue handle peeping out of the top. One single purchase was inside—a popping-balls push-toy vacuum. A note was jotted on the back of the receipt: "For big brother when baby comes."

I looked all around. Not a soul was in sight. However, I suspected that the "angel" I'd just met had left this present. Max never woke up as I hid his gift in my car trunk.

Before I got in to drive, I let out a low volume shriek. First I was giddy and giggling. Then I silently wept a few tears of thanksgiving for the surprise gift my own heavenly Father had planned for this daughter.

Actually, many gifts. Not just a toy, but also answered prayer thanks to help from a wise, kindhearted stranger. I also walked away with the gift of increased confidence regarding my own parental discernment.

I called the store later, but wasn't able to learn who had made that surprise purchase. However, I did learn that I have to exercise tough love by saying no when necessary. It will help my children prepare for their future days of independence when they are old enough to learn on their own, when I just have to "leave 'm here."

God Is Peace

THE RETURN
OF THE REBEL

Mark R. Littleton

I stood looking over the lake as the sun rose, its yellow light glinting off the water like a billion tiny jewels. I had never experienced anything like this before, yet I knew it was the most important thing that had ever happened to me.

Two days earlier I had confessed to a friend that I believed Jesus was the Son of God.

The next twenty-four hours I rode an emotional roller coaster. Abundant joy, exuberant love, and a deep sense of peace and tranquility blew through me like a cool breeze on a steaming night. Everything became a moment of discovery for me. When I picked up a stone, its weight and heft astounded me. Walking barefoot through dewy grass, I felt I had been catapulted into the twilight zone. Prayer was real. When I opened the Bible, it made sense.

My friends and I had driven three hours to my grandparents' lake cabin in the Pocono Mountains of Pennsylvania. As we skied, sailed, swam, and sunned, I worshiped God and relished a totally new feeling of being loved and understood as a person. I was spilling over with joy and just had to tell my friends. I couldn't contain it.

"I just met God—he's real!" I told my best friend, Jon.

"It's eternal life!" I informed Jim and Art.

"Anybody can have it. It's for free! All you have to do is believe!" I said to Bob and Chris and Jeff.

They mostly laughed. "Littleton, you're weird." "Littleton's gone off the deep end this time."

I shrugged it off. They'd see, I was sure.

When it came time to go home, I decided to ride with my parents, who were also at the lake. I wanted to tell them what had happened.

As Dad drove, I talked. I told my parents that the year before I'd read a book about prophecies in the Bible coming true today. After that, I began reading the Bible and praying regularly for nearly nine months. Finally, the previous Thursday, I'd realized I believed in Jesus. After that, an incredible feeling of love, joy, peace, and hope had gripped me—I'd realized that Jesus was now with me, in me, my friend, my Lord, my Master.

"Dad, anybody can have it. All you have to do is believe."

> "You just graduated from college and have good things going for you. Don't blow it now on some feeling."

My mother exclaimed, "Mark, I grew up with people who were into this. It was foolish. They wasted their lives. You just graduated from college and have good things going for you. Don't blow it now on some feeling."

"Mom, it's not a feeling. It's the most real thing I've ever seen."

"There are other things in life that are important too."

"But Mom, what's more important than knowing God, having eternal life, and knowing what happens when you die?"

"I don't think you can know those things just like that," Mom answered. "Pretty soon you'll want me to storm to the altar, weeping about my ridiculous sins!"

I felt as if I were drowning. Didn't anyone understand that knowing Jesus Christ was the greatest thing that could happen to him or her?

"But I'm not afraid anymore. Not afraid of death. Not afraid of the future. I've always been afraid," I explained.

"That's all well and good," my mom said, "just don't push it on everybody."

I wasn't listening. "My self-image too. I've always felt inferior. But now I know God created me the way He did for a reason. I know He loves me and that every part of my personality and being are from Him as a gift."

Both my parents laughed. But I was serious. "Really, my whole life is changed. A week ago I believed in drugs, premarital sex, and drinking. The Bible was just another book, and Jesus was just a good person who gave us a lot of neat quotes. But all of that has changed—in a few days! Look at it this way: what gives *you* peace?"

My mother responded, "Well, when we get home and I see the house is okay, that gives me a real sense of peace."

I thought that was ridiculous. I looked at Dad. "What makes you feel significant, Dad?"

"When I make a sale, I feel like a million dollars." Dad was vice president of sales for a machinery company.

"So it's just about money, then?" I asked.

"No, it's a sense of accomplishment. It's hard work that has paid off."

I shook my head. "All you two think about is material possessions!"

The argument continued for the full three hours of our journey. The nearer we got to home, the more desperate I felt.

As my parents lectured me about reality and discouraged my religious enthusiasm, I began to think in different terms. I would leave home. I would join a group of Christians who lived for Jesus. I could play my guitar and teach others, and we would travel around the world telling people the good news.

When Dad pulled into our driveway, I got out and said, "Dad, I'm leaving."

"What?"

Mom stared at me, furious.

"I can't deal with this anymore. I have to find people who believe in Christ. I'm leaving home."

"Now? At ten o'clock at night?"

I decided not to argue anymore. I started up the street. My father followed me.

"What are you doing? What is this all about?"

"Dad, I don't think you know what life is all about."

He argued with me, coaxed me, and begged me. I fought off every plea. He shook his head with frustration. "Then you won't come home?"

"No."

I turned to go. Dad watched me, and then I heard him turn back for home.

I wandered around, praying that God would work some miracle to show my parents the truth. I decided to visit my friends, the Pezzis, who had originally talked to me about Jesus.

It was midnight on Sunday night when I reached the Pezzis' house, but they were still up, watching television. Mr. and Mrs. Pezzi invited me in, and I told them all that had happened. They were glad to know I'd given my life to Jesus, but they didn't know what to tell me about leaving home. Finally, Mrs. Pezzi called her friend Betsy to come by and counsel me.

Betsy went through the plan of salvation using a little pamphlet. As she laid it out, I kept saying, "Right. That's what I believe. That's what I've done."

Finally, she came to what had happened that night with my parents.

"Mark, do you know the Ten Commandments?" she asked, gazing into my eyes.

God Is Peace

"Sort of."

She opened her Bible to Exodus 20 and read them to me. When she reached the fifth one, she paused, "Honor your father and your mother." Then she asked, "Do you think that's what you did tonight?"

I bowed my head. "No, I guess I didn't."

She told me to go back home and ask for forgiveness. That was the only way I could demonstrate that I had truly changed. And then I had to begin the hard work of honoring my parents each day after.

I gulped, thinking that Mom and Dad might not even let me in the house.

> She told me to go back home and ask for forgiveness. That was the only way I could demonstrate that I had truly changed.

Betsy assured me, "God is with you, Mark. He will lead you. Nothing that has happened is unrecoverable. God allowed this tonight for reasons you may never know. But He's there, and He's making sure you go down the right path."

I had never heard such a thing. But in my spirit, the idea resonated. If I had a relationship now with the glorious God of the universe, didn't it make sense that He would guide me, advise me, and lead me through the days and problems of life? Excitement filled me as I realized God really was involved in my life and that I could trust Him.

To my surprise, even though it was 3:00 a.m., the back door to the house wasn't locked. I went straight to my parents' bedroom. When I opened the door, Dad jumped out of bed. "Thank God you're home!" he said, hugging me hard.

I stammered out my apology.

"Don't worry about it. These things happen. I love you," he said, with his arm over my shoulder.

It was the first time in my life that my dad had ever said those words to me. It was a touching, potent moment.

Mom got up, and they both walked me to my bedroom. She said, "We love you, honey. Don't ever forget that." I learned later they had been driving around, looking for me on the street and even praying that I would be okay.

As I stood by my bed, I asked that we pray together. They agreed, and I said, "Lord, help me to honor my parents and help them to understand what has happened. Thanks. Amen."

Dad hugged me again. "Get some sleep. You've got a big day tomorrow." I did. I was supposed to start a new job.

That night I lay in bed marveling. So much seemed to be happening inside me in such a short time. In a way, I felt frightened.

As I reflected on the evening, though, I knew God had been with me every step of the way that night. I realized He would never desert me, even when I messed up badly.

Later, I would memorize a verse that summed it up perfectly: "The Lord directs the steps of the godly. He delights in every detail of their lives. Though they stumble, they will never fall, for the Lord holds them by the hand" (Psalm 37:23–24).

I fell asleep with a deepening sense that an adventure had begun that would never end. I'd just experienced the presence of God in my life at a level I'd never seen, but something inside told me this would become the normal, rich, stunning experience in the days ahead.

God Is Peace

EXCLUSIVE BONUS CONTENT FROM GUIDEPOSTS

Read on for more true stories of
answered prayer . . . exclusive to
this Guideposts edition!

RESCUE FROM A RAGING INFERNO

Terry Burleson

On the plains of northwest Oklahoma, you can see for miles: nothing but prairie grass, clumps of cedar trees, and rugged red-rock canyons. But even with my binoculars, I could barely make out the helicopters, one after the other, dumping water on a wildfire at the horizon. I wasn't concerned by the small plume of smoke snaking skyward. It had to be at least fifty miles away, across the South Canadian River.

That afternoon, my uncle Larry, cousin Tony, and I had driven to this four-thousand-acre ranch for a planned three days of turkey hunting. Larry had brought three horses for us to use, moseying about the ranch like real cowpokes. At age fifty-seven, I was semiretired from a career in retail management. It felt great to get away for some male bonding.

I snapped a few pictures of the bushy cedars and the canyon rims—nothing but blue skies above—and texted them to my wife, Ande, two hours away. "Nothing to worry about," I typed. "Having a great time." She'd seen the fire on the news and called a few minutes earlier to warn me, but we'd lost the cell connection. I didn't want her fretting. I knew she'd be praying regardless. All that talking-to-God stuff came harder for me. It was hard to imagine him actually listening to anything I'd have to say.

The wind had picked up, blowing hard from the southwest. We left the horses in the stable by the ranch house and climbed into a Gator utility vehicle, with Larry driving, to scout for places to draw out the gobblers the next day. We headed north on a small gravel road that hugged the ranch perimeter. We stopped here and there to look for signs of turkeys.

We drove for about a mile before Larry turned to head back south, toward the ranch house. As we did, my eyes went wide. A wall of flames was racing toward us, maybe three-quarters of a mile away.

"Get us out of here!" I screamed. Larry whipped around, bouncing hard over the gravel road. How had the fire jumped the river? To cover that kind of ground so fast would have taken tornado-like speed. The flames would be on us in no time.

"What about the horses?"

"What about our trucks?"

"How can we save ourselves?"

We weren't expecting answers. We were just trying to keep from totally losing it. I looked back. Amazingly, we were gaining on the fire.

Until we ran out of road.

A heavy-duty barbed-wire fence blocked the way. There was no way to get the Gator past it. Larry, Tony, and I jumped off and scrambled to the other side. But it hardly mattered. On foot, we were goners. I called Ande.

"We're surrounded by fire," I shouted over the howling wind. "Call 911! We need a helicopter to get us out of here." The connection went dead.

I looked around. Where were Larry and Tony? The smoke was so thick, I couldn't see more than a few feet around me. I yelled for the other guys. All I could hear were the cedars exploding. The dry grass crackled like popcorn. It was terrifying. I reached in my pocket for my cell phone again. Gone. I must have dropped it. That phone was my only contact with the outside world. But there was no time to look further.

I stumbled blindly, choking from the smoke. Flames reached out and tagged me, burning my clothes. If I didn't get some fresh air, I was going to die of smoke inhalation. I knelt down, my face near the ground, gasping for breath.

I'd never needed God as I did now. But I never felt as if I'd done anything to deserve His help or His love. Ande was up every morning at 5:30, praying and reading the Bible. Me? I'd put nearly everything else in my life first—work, family, chores. The only times God had felt real to me were Sunday mornings. For years I'd driven two hours every other weekend to look after my mother and mow her property. Driving home, I'd turn the radio to a station out of Tulsa that played old-time gospel music, those wide-open Oklahoma skies spreading out before me. I felt as if I was in the arms of the Creator. I never got that feeling anywhere else.

I was on my own here. Through the smoke, the flames biting me every step of the way, I made it to the top of a canyon. For the moment, I was above the fire. To the west, maybe a quarter mile away, I saw a flat area the fire hadn't reached, a place clear of cedars.

I half-ran, half-staggered there, then collapsed on the ground. I took deep breaths. After a few minutes, I tried to stand. Smoke filled my lungs. I fell back to the ground. Behind me came a roar like a freight train. I looked back. All I could see were towering flames.

I pulled myself to my feet. I went one way, then another, the blaze chasing me. Somehow I ended up in an area that had already been burned, the ground charred black. How I'd gotten there, I had no idea. It was as if I'd been carried. I lay on the embers—my scalp, my back burning, blistering. I didn't even have the strength to lift my head.

"God, please let me live," I cried out in desperation. It was the first prayer I'd said in years. I knew it was too late to expect any favors from God. I only hoped he'd be there for Ande. "Let her know I love her," I whispered.

Hot wind whipped dirt and ash against me. The fire would be right behind it, burning over me. I dug into my pocket and found a handkerchief; I put it over my nose and mouth. Closed my eyes tight. A peace came over me. I was ready to die. I just hoped I'd lose consciousness before the flames reached me. A minute passed. Then two. I opened my eyes as much as I dared. The flames had burned a kind of firebreak into the ground just yards away from me. Now it was blowing away from me. A miracle.

I stood and started walking, no idea of the direction I was going. It looked like a war zone, blackened cedars littering the countryside. Was anybody searching for me? I hadn't seen a single helicopter. In the distance I saw a windmill and a large, round stock tank on a concrete slab, a place where I could lie down, away from burning embers. It took every bit of strength I had left, but I got there just as darkness fell.

I dipped my handkerchief in the cool water I found, washing soot and ash off my face and wetting my lips. Water, even though it wasn't the cleanest, had never tasted so good.

I collapsed onto the concrete. The air was still smoky. How much more could I breathe in before it killed me? Would I even live till morning? I wished I'd been able to tell Ande and my kids how much I loved them. In the distance, I watched as cedars burst like fireworks, the fire ravaging everything in its path. The flames had surrounded me—by any logic, the fire should have consumed me too. And yet, as if a shield protected me, I'd been spared its full fury.

I looked up. Helicopter lights zipped across the sky. But there was no second pass. No one had seen me. I stared up at the majestic starry heavens. The view went on forever, beyond what my eyes could possibly take in. The only thing I could compare it to were those drives back from my mom's. That overwhelming sense of God's presence. He'd been with me then. He'd shielded me from the flames today. He would be with me always. I didn't have to do anything to earn his love. I thought of Ande's prayers, the prayers of folks at church she had no doubt asked for. I felt their love too. There on the hard concrete, without another soul around, I felt watched over, a feeling I'd never known before.

"Thank you, Lord," I prayed. "For never giving up on me. Thank you for Ande and the kids, for the life you've given me." The words came freely, easily, as if I were talking to an old friend. I talked to him all night, about everything I could think of, making up for lost time.

At sunup, I started walking. Before long, I saw a pickup. Two men got out.

"Have you been out here all night?" one asked. "We were just going to work at the oil rig, but we'll make sure you get help. You're one lucky dude."

"Do you have any water?" I was downing my third bottle when a silver SUV pulled up. My son, Jordan, and sons-in-law, Mark and Sean, and my good friend Don got out. "He's alive!" they shouted. One of them held a phone to my ear. "Everything's going to be okay," Ande said. "I love you."

The boys explained that Larry and Tony were safe. The horses had survived as well. A helicopter took me to the burn unit in Oklahoma City. As it lifted off, I took one last look at the charred landscape below. Total devastation. More than 280,000 acres would burn. But in the blackness I saw hope, the promise of a new day dawning, new growth.

I was alive because the fire had miraculously changed direction. And so had I.

HOOKED

Gladys Fullerton

$\mathcal{I}$t gets pretty hot in the summer out in Lakeland, Oklahoma. One real scorcher four years ago, I invited my granddaughter Kasey, who was visiting, to come fishing with me. "Maybe later," she said. "It's too hot right now."

She wasn't the only one who didn't want to go. It wasn't a good day for fishing, or so the "real" fishermen who were hanging around the bait shop told me. "It's a hundred degrees, lady! All the fish have headed for deeper water to cool off." I ignored them. I was ninety years old, used to making my own decisions, especially about fishing. So I bought a bucket of minnows and headed to the marina with my gear.

I crossed the swinging bridge and went into the little building where I'd set up for the day. It was cooler there, with a nice breeze coming off the water. I tied up the basket for my catch over in the usual corner, then laid out a towel to wrap around any fish who flopped around too much. *I'll use two poles today,* I decided. Someone had given me a comfortable chair. I settled down in it and cast my lines.

Maybe those naysayers had been right. The fish weren't biting. Didn't matter to me; I still had a good time. I listened to the waves splash against the dock and a woodpecker working away on a tree somewhere. The bright-blue sky and puffy white clouds and water as far as I could see soothed my soul. My mind wandered, and I thought of something I'd read recently: "God wants to do more than we ask."

Maybe I could ask him to catch me a fish, I thought. But I couldn't. It seemed disrespectful and inappropriate. I thought some more. It would be okay to ask for a fish for someone else, wouldn't it? "God, my granddaughter is visiting, as you know, and I would kinda like to show off by catching just one big crappie. Surely there's a big one down there." I said it right out loud, which is okay to do if you're alone. At my age, I'd learned to be careful about that, though, because if someone heard me talking to myself they'd say, "Oh, bless her, that poor thing. She's losing it."

My thoughts were drifting off again when suddenly I felt something: a tug on my line. There it was again! I reeled it in. A beautiful crappie! I kept going, heat or no heat. And I kept reeling them in, one after another, till the basket in the corner was stuffed with nine of the biggest crappies I'd ever caught!

Right about then I felt the swinging bridge move, so I knew someone was coming. It was Kasey. "Hi, Grandma," she said. "Catch anything?"

I tried to be nonchalant. "Pretty good day," I told her, pointing to the basket in the corner. She went over to look for herself. In a voice loud enough that everyone in Lakeland could have heard, she said, "I can't believe it! You caught nine crappies! And they're huge!"

So I suppose this is a story about the ones that *didn't* get away. Sure, my prayer was about fishing. But God's answer, as always, was about so much more.

GOD ALWAYS PROVIDES

Cheryl Morgan

$\mathcal{I}$ sat at our small kitchen table, working on a list of the things we'd need for the adoption of four children from the Philippines. Our family was about to double in size. *Prioritize!* I told myself.

A larger kitchen table was definitely a priority. Unless we were planning to eat in shifts, we'd need to find seating for eight. I penciled that in, under my note for the extra freezer we'd need to store the massive amounts of food we somehow had to buy. We needed bunk beds, a minivan so we could fit the whole family in one car. The list seemed endless. *How would we ever manage?*

I'd started praying about adoption almost three years earlier, after a miscarriage. Our children, Amy and Matthew, were 10 and 7. I couldn't shake the feeling that Jeff and I were meant to bring another child into our family. And finally, earlier this year, I felt a conviction that now was the time. I'd written in my journal the letters "p.a." for *pursue adoption*, because adopting even one child seemed so overwhelming that I couldn't bring myself to write out the actual words. But I did tell a few friends what was on my heart.

One friend had recently been to the Philippines to visit her sister, who was working in an orphanage.

"There is a wonderful little girl there who is up for adoption," she told me. "Her name is Annabel."

Perfect, a little girl! I thought.

"And she has three older brothers," she added.

"Four kids! We can't adopt four kids."

"They're so sweet," she said. "Their mother died when Annabel was just a year old. Their father was disabled and felt they'd be best cared for at the orphanage." She showed me a newsletter that had photos of the children. As I stared at the photo, time seemed to stand still. I knew that God meant for these children to join our family.

How exactly we were going to make that happen was unclear. My husband, Jeff, worked as a youth minister and was studying at seminary at night. Our family budget was stretched to the max. Plus, how would the family dynamic change? Could we meet the needs of not just one child who'd lost their birth parents, but four? How would Amy and Matthew adjust?

That night, I told Jeff about the four siblings in the Philippines who needed a home. No, not just a home. A *family*. We discussed it over the weekend. He was having the same concerns I was. But that Monday night, he returned home from school with confidence.

"I was praying about the adoption," he said. "And I heard God speak to me. He said: 'Haven't I always provided?' I think we should do this."

We dove right in. First, we told our kids, who were thrilled. We applied for the adoption and filled out reams of forms required by the state of Minnesota and the Philippine government. Jeff and I were fingerprinted for a background check, and we scheduled a home visit to be interviewed. We attended a seminar on parenting adopted children. We talked about how we'd organize the kids' bedrooms: one for the boys, one for the girls.

Now, seven months after we started the process, we'd just been approved! It was September, and we'd be going to the Philippines in November to bring our four new additions home. I was over the moon—and completely overwhelmed.

I stared at the too-small kitchen table again. It had been in Jeff's family since he was a kid. But it would fit only six at the most. It just wouldn't work. To me, it symbolized this whole crazy notion. I wanted to trust in those words that God had told Jeff, but with this unfinished list in front of me, I was finding that difficult.

A few days later, my mother called. "The neighbors are selling their freezer. I'll buy it for you if you want."

"Yes, that is one thing I've been praying for," I said. I was grateful, but I didn't think too much about it, until the next call. A mother I knew.

"Do you like beef?"

"Sure we do," I said. It seemed like such an odd question.

"Do you have a big freezer?"

"Well," I said, "we will soon."

"Oh good," she said. "Because I felt led to buy you two hundred and fifty pounds of beef."

Haven't I always provided? The words echoed in my mind. I had wanted a freezer. But the meat to fill it? That wasn't even on my list.

A day later, my phone rang again. A friend I'd worked with years before. "Do you need a big table? My husband found one at an estate sale, but it's too big for our dining room."

Calls and offers kept coming in. An older minivan we could afford. Three sets of bunk beds. By November, every item on my list was accounted for. We flew to the Philippines and after four days came home to frigid Minnesota, a family of eight.

The first night back, we sat down at the table big enough for all of us. The kids talked and laughed over pizza. I glanced at Jeff and squeezed his hand. It was clear. This was going to work out just fine. God always provides.

RESCUE PSALM 91

Dewayne Parish

*O*klahoma was my new home now that I was retired from my pastoral work, but as my wife, Ann, and I watched the news one night, I felt more like we were living in Egypt during the time of the ten plagues. "Another hailstorm," I groaned when we saw the warning scroll by at the bottom of the television screen.

"Oh, no!" Ann said.

I looked up sadly, thinking of our roof. Just that afternoon I'd admired it gleaming in the sun. It ought to gleam—it was practically brand new. Our third new roof in four years, in fact. Each one had been destroyed by brutal Oklahoma hail driven by raging wind. Chunks of ice the size of softballs had dinged the shingles, smashed the vents and destroyed the guttering. *Not again*, I thought. *Please.*

"A hailstorm is on its way toward Oklahoma City," the weatherman confirmed. According to the weather map, we had forty-five minutes until it was right on top of us.

There was nothing more we could do to prepare. We'd already bought the strongest roof we could find. Once that was in place, I'd anointed the home with oil and prayed over the whole parameter of our property, asking God to send angels to protect it. I watched the rest of the news and checked the clock. Thirty minutes to go before our new roof and my prayers would be put to the test.

I flipped to another TV station, hoping to hear that the storm had changed direction, but it was bearing down ever closer. Twenty minutes. Ten. It was time to bring out the big guns. "I'm going to pray Psalm 91," I told Ann. I stepped outside the front door. Heavy gray clouds filled the night sky to the northwest. I could already hear the hail coming, hitting everything in its path. I recited from memory: "I dwell in the secret place of the most high and abide under the shadow of the Almighty. I say of the Lord, you are my refuge and my fortress; my God in whom I trust."

The storm advanced like an invading army, the clouds rolling across the sky above our heads. Hail pelted the roof. Ann walked out to stand with me. "You will deliver us from the snare of the fowler and the deadly pestilence." I imagined the Angel of the Lord spreading his wings out over our property. That would protect us for sure. "You will cover us with your feathers, and under your wings shall we trust."

By now I was practically shouting over the storm. The sky was so dark I could barely see anything very clearly. But out in the yard, something dropped from that sky. Not hail, birds. Great big birds, gray and white, with black heads and wingspans three feet across. "I've never seen such a bird," Ann said.

Nor had I. A whole flock descended on our lawn, perhaps a hundred or more. The birds landed on the grass, covering every inch. They tucked their heads under their wings for cover. The hail stopped. The storm moved off. The world went quiet. The birds untucked their heads from their wings. Together they flew off into the sky. Ann and I went back inside. We decided that tomorrow would be soon enough to assess the damage.

The next morning dawned bright and sunny. "Let's do this together," Ann said. We stepped into the yard.

"I don't believe it," I said. Our roof gleamed in the sun, looking brand new. Not a ding or a missing shingle. The gutters were sound. Even the vegetable garden was untouched. I could see I'd be giving out the number of our roofer to my neighbors. And I had a very good book I'd highly recommend as well.

Beyond Help?

Judith Hayes

$\mathcal{I}$'d never seen an angrier man. Arms folded, gaze fixed on the carpet of the hotel ballroom—Earl was by far the most unpromising participant among the hundred couples who had come to the marriage-counseling seminar. And I was stuck with him in my morning breakout group. His face wore a defiant scowl. His wife, Kim, wiped her teary eyes and dabbed at her cheeks with a tissue.

"I just want us to be happy," she said. "He's always so angry."

Earl unfolded his arms briefly to scratch the stubble on his chin, but he never looked up at Kim or anyone else. I'd begun the weekend-long seminar hoping I could help everyone I counseled. And we'd had plenty of successes—most of the couples were able to start talking, and listening, to each other again. Others learned that a small act of kindness—like offering to get their spouses a cup of water or coffee, or even giving a hug—could start the healing process.

But Earl and Kim? Their marriage seemed doomed. I hurt so much for Kim. Her energy was gentle, loving, soft. Her husband's energy was, well, volcanic.

I tried to draw Earl out with some basic questions about himself and his marriage. "What is this, the Spanish Inquisition?" he shouted, glaring at me.

"See what I mean?" Kim said. "He shouts all the time. He's so defensive. I can't take it anymore."

I was grateful when the morning session came to an end. We wrapped up with a moment of prayer. I closed my eyes and bowed my head. As unpleasant as Earl had been, I prayed for him. *Lord, how can I help someone who is so enraged?*

My eyes remained closed, but something appeared in front of me. The strangest image: a fuzzy brown teddy bear with a plaid bow around its neck. I shook my head to clear my mind.

At lunch, I ate with my husband, Mike, who had sat in on the group and witnessed the whole troubling session. After a few bites I put down my sandwich and leaned close to him. "I know this will sound crazy," I whispered, "but I think I'm supposed to buy Earl a teddy bear."

I explained the vision. How I was out of ideas on how to help this couple. My husband rolled his eyes. "All right. Let's go find a teddy bear."

Fortunately, a store nearby had a large display of teddy bears. I waded through pink teddy bears, white teddy bears, and black teddy bears. Some were holding blankets or baby teddy bears or red satin hearts. At last I found a brown bear with fuzzy fur and a plaid bow. Would it help Earl? Or would I end up rescuing it from the trash can?

The seminar resumed and the couples and counselors regrouped. I walked toward the back, where Earl was hiding out, the teddy bear in a brown paper bag under my arm. "Earl? I've got something for you," I said. He barely acknowledged me. I handed him the bag and walked away.

Minutes later, one of the lead counselors stood at the podium at the front of the room and cleared his throat. "Would anyone like to share something they learned in their sessions this morning?" he asked.

Someone stood and moved toward the microphone. The last person I would have expected. Earl had the bear clutched to his chest; his shoulders were clenched. Was he going to explode?

He said nothing at first. His eyes brimmed with tears. Finally he took a deep breath, composed himself, and began to tell his story.

He'd grown up with an abusive father, a man who beat him for every infraction, no matter how slight. Once, as punishment for something, his father grabbed Earl's beloved teddy bear, marched the boy out to the backyard and threw the bear into the trash incinerator—forcing Earl to watch. My heart ached for Earl—the little boy and the man he'd become.

Earl held up the teddy bear. "God knew I needed this," he said into the microphone. "To remember where my anger comes from. My wife doesn't deserve it. No one does."

He left the podium then, locking eyes with Kim. They met and held each other close, the teddy bear between them.

JONATHAN'S HEART

Lori Wood

I first met Jonathan Pinkard in December 2018. The day started normally. I walked into Piedmont Newnan Hospital in Newnan, Georgia, where I worked as an ICU nurse. When I arrived, my coworker told me about Jonathan, one of the patients I'd be caring for that day. He was an autistic twenty-six-year-old with no home address, and he'd been in and out of the local hospitals since August.

Although he was in heart failure, he'd been removed from the transplant list because he wasn't able to take care of himself. He couldn't remember to take his medicine regularly. He didn't eat right. His PICC line—the intravenous tube used to administer medication—was always coming out. Without someone to help him manage his care, he wouldn't be able to get back on the transplant list. "There's no one to help him," my coworker said. "His mom has health problems and lives in a nursing home. He never knew his dad. His grandmother raised him, but he's been on his own ever since she died."

I shook my head and went into Jonathan's room. When I got there, he was clearly agitated. "Why is this happening to me?" he said. "I'm hungry, and they won't let me eat."

I checked his chart. "You're having your PICC line reinserted, and you can't eat until after the procedure is over." He was so upset that I called and requested that they take him sooner. I couldn't fix much for Jonathan, but at least I could make sure he got lunch.

When he was moved out of the ICU and onto the regular-care floor, I checked in on him before and after my shifts. Jonathan was a sweet young man, and we had some common interests. His favorite show was Family Feud. I watched it every night. We both loved college football. I rooted for the University of Georgia Bulldogs, and he was a fan of the University of Alabama Crimson Tide, and we had some lively discussions about the rivalry between the teams.

His situation pulled at my heartstrings. He'd been given a death sentence and he hadn't done anything wrong. What if he were one of my sons? I knew what I had to do. After all, I was a nurse and had an extra bedroom.

I sat down with my youngest son, Austin, and told him about Jonathan. My oldest had moved out long ago, and my middle son, Ryan, was away at college, but Austin still lived at home. He would have to deal with the most change. "I know it's a lot, but Jonathan will die unless someone helps him," I said. "I think God wants me to be that someone." I waited for his response. God had called me to do this, and I didn't want anyone to try to change my mind.

But Austin did no such thing. "Of course, Mom," he said. "You have to do this. You're the perfect person to help him out."

I breathed a sigh of relief, then called Ryan to let him know what was happening. "Jonathan would move into your room and you'd have to sleep on the couch when you came home," I warned him.

"That's no problem. I can tell this is important to you," Ryan said.

To get Jonathan's name back on the transplant list, I had to agree to be his full-time caregiver if a heart became available for the surgery. I had to sign a document promising to be with Jonathan twenty-four hours a day, seven days a week for the first month after the surgery. In order for me to be approved for an extended medical leave from work, Jonathan had to be a family member. I applied to become his temporary legal guardian, but he had already taken to calling me Mama. I was nervous about having to defend my position, but everything went off without a hitch. I was granted guardianship and the necessary family medical leave from work. For the next few months, I kept our situation as private as possible, praying for a heart for Jonathan.

On May 23, 2019, Jonathan was admitted to the hospital for a heart biopsy. Without a transplant, he had as little as six months to live. He was running out of time. I sat down on the edge of his hospital bed, hoping I had the right words. "You have an important decision to make," I told him. I explained that doctors wanted to surgically implant a left ventricle assist device, or LVAD, in his chest. I feared he wasn't grasping the gravity of the situation, even though it was far from a perfect solution. The battery lasted for only fourteen hours at a time. It had to be connected to power overnight, and we lived out in the country where the electricity sometimes went out. Then there were potential post-op complications of strokes or infections. But it was Jonathan's decision. He refused the LVAD. My prayers for a new heart went into overdrive.

On the first of August, I got the call—a heart was available. Jonathan's transplant surgery lasted eight hours. I spent the night in the waiting room, praying. "God, you've gotten him this far," I murmured. "Be with him now."

When the doctors finally came out and told me everything had gone well, I nearly wept with relief.

Ten days later, Jonathan came home to recover. Most of what he needed was guidance. I reminded him to take his antirejection medications four times a day. I took him to his weekly medical appointments. I taught him how to find and prepare low-sodium recipes and encouraged him to exercise. I wanted to teach Jonathan how to take care of himself so he could be independent.

Little by little, Jonathan regained his strength. After the first month, I had to return to work, but I didn't need to worry. Austin was there with Jonathan when I wasn't. His help was invaluable, and I couldn't believe how selflessly he gave of his time.

We watched Jonathan learn new things. When I was at work, he'd text me links to low-sodium recipes he wanted to try. When I got home in the evening, he was waiting for me on the front porch, ready to tell me about the progress he'd made that day.

Soon Jonathan was well enough to move out and start living on his own. God orchestrated everything to heal Jonathan, beyond anything I could have asked for. No one had questioned my instinct to do what I could to help a young man in need. Everyone had stepped up to smooth the process along, and I learned something wonderful: the world expects us to help one another.

GOD'S GRACE
AND A BANJO

Don Embry

I pulled a piece of curly maple from a stack at the specialty wood shop. I checked its color, its grain, its sturdiness. This would be the neck of the banjo I was building. It needed to be exactly right. To feel right in my hands, right from the start.

I'd built dozens of banjos over the years, but this one was different. You could say my life's story would be in this banjo. A lifetime of mistakes, self-destruction, and redemption. I wanted this banjo to tell that story, to share my truth, every time it was played.

At last I found the perfect piece. I loaded it into my truck and headed for my workshop at home.

* * *

I grew up outside Washington, DC, not far from where I now live in Virginia. It wasn't a happy childhood. My dad was a quiet man, a hard worker. But when he drank, he became mean.

I was terrified of ending up like him. As soon as I was old enough, I joined the Marines. The Vietnam War was on, and I landed in the middle of it.

My tour lasted thirteen months. I came home haunted by what I'd seen over there. Haunted too by a question: Why did I make it back when so many of my friends didn't?

I hadn't realized how strongly public opinion had turned against the war. The first time I went out wearing my uniform, I was taunted and spat on. In the eyes of some people, I was a monster, a killer. I didn't know what to think. I had served my country. But I'd also witnessed horrific suffering. Death and destruction. I put my Marine uniform away. I would try to forget all about Vietnam and just move on with my life.

* * *

I unloaded the piece of curly maple from my truck and took it to the workshop I'd built behind my house. I set it on a band saw and cut it into the right shape, inhaling the sweet scent of the wood. I sanded it smooth and added a tinted finish, bringing out the rippled pattern in the grain.

* * *

I worked odd jobs after the war—gas station attendant, electric company technician. I'd gotten married just before the war, and we had two daughters. I wanted a quiet, normal life.

Then my wife got in a car accident. The man I'd become after Vietnam was no good at caregiving. We eventually divorced. I left my family and barely stayed in touch with my daughters.

I found work as an auto mechanic in Annandale, Virginia. One day at lunch, the shop foreman pulled a fiddle from a case and another worker got out a guitar.

"Do you play anything?" the foreman asked me.

"No," I said. I loved music but had never learned an instrument.

"We could use a banjo," said the foreman.

The two of them struck up a tune, and something happened inside me. The anguish I'd carried from Vietnam eased. The music was like a salve. I watched and listened, hypnotized by their finger work. Everything went away except the music.

I bought a cheap banjo and taught myself to play. To my delight, music seemed to come naturally. Soon I was playing with the guys at the shop and any chance I got at home.

Our little group got some gigs at bars. We'd play, then stay to drink. Music and booze—what a combination! It blotted out my war memories and my guilt, how I'd treated my family, feelings that boiled right up when the music stopped.

I looked forward to those gigs. In between, I drank alone at home. I'd become just like my dad.

* * *

Once the neck of the banjo was complete, I ordered the metal parts from a supplier I trusted in Europe—the tone ring, tension hoop, brackets, tail pieces and tuners. I affixed them to an intact banjo head I'd found online. The only thing left to do was to put everything together, attach the strings, and add decorative insignia to the head and neck.

* * *

For years, my life zigzagged between drunkenness and fitful attempts to start over. I drifted away from the auto shop and the band and stowed my banjo in a closet. I worked construction, remarried, bought some land in Maryland, and built a house.

My second wife, Sandi, urged me to join the VFW. She thought talking with other veterans might help. I went to a couple meetings, but hearing other guys talk just brought up the painful memories I'd tried to bury. I came home wanting to get drunk.

Sandi was patient and loving, but she grew dismayed when I relapsed after a rehab program. We separated, and I cursed myself for having ruined another marriage.

I lost my job during the 2008 recession. I drank even more.

"You have to stop drinking, Don," my doctor said. "You have Stage III cirrhosis. You're going to die."

I drank anyway.

One day, I stumbled out of my stupor long enough to discover a notice of imminent foreclosure in the mail. I was practically broke and had stopped making house payments.

Desperate, I called my older daughter, Dawn. She was grown now, working in real estate. She wasn't happy to hear from me—we barely talked. But she agreed to help me out of daughterly duty. "We'll sell your house before it forecloses and use the money to buy something smaller," she said. I felt ashamed.

We went together to look at one of those smaller houses. Dawn walked inside, but I stopped on the porch.

"You go on in without me," I said. "I need a minute."

I was so sick, just getting out of the car had exhausted me. I stood there feeling utterly defeated. No money. Twice divorced. Estranged from my kids. About to lose the house I'd built myself. Dawn had been buying me food. Even now, all I could think about was my next drink.

There was only one word to describe me: *failure.*

"God," I whispered, "please help me."

Why did I say that? I wasn't a praying man. Yet at that moment, those words felt like my only lifeline, a crease of light in a door that was about to close forever.

I can't explain what happened next. It was like that moment when the guys played in the auto shop, except on a whole different scale. All of the hatred and disgust I'd felt with myself just melted away. It was quite literally a physical sensation of release, a collapse of all my defenses. I felt vulnerable yet protected.

God didn't excuse what I'd done. He let me know he loved me nonetheless, maybe even more for my brokenness, and forgave me. Unconditionally, so I could forgive myself. I had no choice but to accept that love, that grace. It filled up all the painful places I used to try to drown with alcohol. I felt staggered by a sense of relief. I wept.

"Dad?" Dawn said. "Are you okay? Do you need a drink?"

I was startled to hear myself say, "No."

* * *

The banjo head arrived. I used my lathe to cut a wooden rim for it, then attached it to the neck. All that remained was the pearl inlay. I'd sent a design to a man I knew in Kentucky. This design was special. It would set this banjo apart from every other one I'd made.

* * *

After that day on the porch, my life unfolded in what I can only describe as a series of miracles. No longer poisoned by alcohol, my liver healed. I bought a small house in Virginia and found work in construction. For the first time since Vietnam, I allowed myself to ask why I'd survived. In other words, what should I do with this life God had given to me?

The answer came in the form of a memory. My old banjo. I found it in the closet. I tuned it but hesitated before picking and strumming. Would I remember? I tried a few chords. I could still play!

But where? Not bars. I needed a different kind of place.

Just a few days later, I was on the phone with a friend when he mentioned a church gospel group that needed a banjo player.

"Well, I'm a banjo player who's been praying for a gospel group," I said.

I started playing at the church every Sunday. Standing in front of that congregation, making beautiful music for God, I felt as if I'd come home.

It wasn't long before I was making my own banjos. I wanted a life filled with music.

* * *

The pearl inlay design arrived. I pulled it out of the box.

The inlay consisted of four words, *United States Marine Corps*, alongside the eagle, globe, and anchor of the Marine emblem, which I layered onto the head of the banjo, and a few smaller pieces representing Marine ranks that I used to decorate the neck. This banjo was a tribute to the Marines. A symbol of my intention to embrace my time in the service. I planned to play it at an upcoming Veterans Day picnic. I was pretty nervous about this particular debut.

I arrived at the picnic and made my way through a crowd of vets and their families to a stage where I would join a volunteer band. I knew what would happen next. People would want to see the banjo. They'd want to talk, to share their memories. The banjo would make it impossible for me to duck out.

We played a set, and the audience applauded. Afterward people came up to get a closer look at the banjo.

"It's beautiful," said one of the folks standing near me. "Where'd you get it?"

"Made it myself."

Soon I was surrounded. The banjo opened up conversations, honest talk about war. My conflicted feelings about Vietnam turned out to be not so uncommon. War leaves no one unscarred. We are broken by war but made whole by grace.

"Can I take a photo of your banjo?" a woman asked. "It's for my husband. He's a Marine in Afghanistan. It will make him so happy to see this."

Him and me both.

After the picnic, I climbed into my truck and headed home. The banjo lay on the seat beside me. It was the truth teller I had hoped it would be. And at last, so was I.

The Divine Nudge that Brought Me Home

Joanie Smith

A friend and I had just finished having dinner at our favorite spot in Reno, Nevada, where I'd lived for twenty-three years. We paid the bill, got up, and hugged in a tearful goodbye. She was the last friend I'd see before I moved across the country.

"Are you sure about this, Joanie?" she asked. "What is there for you in West Virginia?"

It was a question I couldn't answer. I'd simply woken up one morning in early February with an undeniable urge to return to Huntington, West Virginia. I asked God why. In Reno, I had friends, a business—a full life. The only person I knew in Huntington now was my mother, and she and I didn't get along.

When I was growing up, I never felt close to my mom. She was guarded around me. She hardly ever hugged me or held my hand. She was distant and bitter, often keeping to herself and watching TV in her sewing room. At fifteen years old, I learned that she'd been diagnosed with paranoid schizophrenia. That may have explained her behavior, but for a daughter who wanted to know her mother's love, the diagnosis didn't erase the hurt her behavior had caused. My father loved us both and had always hoped that Mom and I would somehow develop a real relationship. Dad had died without seeing it come to pass. I couldn't imagine it ever happening.

"I can't explain it," I told my friend. "I just know I have to go."

I'd arranged to stay with my mother while I looked for my own place. I'd sold my business and given away most of my possessions, and now I'd said goodbye to my friends. I packed up my Saturn and drove some 2,290 miles to Huntington. When I finally arrived, I walked up to the door with my suitcase and rang the bell. Mom answered, stone-faced. She eyed me up and down.

"Oh, it's you," she said.

She let me in and led me to my old room. *What am I doing here?*

Over the next month, I settled into my new life and found an apartment nearby. I visited almost every day out of a sense of duty. Mom and I fell into a kind of routine. I'd come over with food, work in her garden. One day I joined her in the sewing room, where we sat quietly, watching TV.

"I had a dream about your father," Mom said out of the blue. She went on to explain. She'd been standing here, in the sewing room, when Dad walked in. He took her hand and sat her down in her armchair. Then he grabbed another chair and put it in front of her, facing her. "Wait here," he said in her dream. "I'm going to get Joanie." He left the room, and Mom woke up. It was more than she'd revealed to me about anything since I'd arrived.

"When did you have this dream?" I asked.

"Back in early February," she said, "before I knew you were coming."

The same time I felt my urge. Mom retreated into her shell before I could tell her. She didn't mention the dream again, and I didn't ask about it. She'd never shared anything so personal with me before. I didn't want to ruin it by prying.

Our visits continued, unchanged. Until Mom's forgetfulness became alarming. I took her to the doctor, who diagnosed her with dementia. Because I was the only family she had and we had a steady routine, the best solution was for me to move back in. I became her full-time caregiver.

As Mom's dementia progressed, her guardedness fell away. She became sweet and easy to get along with. We talked more and even laughed together. She spoke a lot about when she was younger, as if she were reliving those days. She mentioned her sister, Margaret, a lot. I knew Margaret had died when my mom was in her early twenties, before schizophrenia took over her life. Perhaps I was seeing Mom as she was back then, as the woman she used to be. The possibility filled me with a new kind of compassion for her.

One day, I went to ask Mom what she wanted for lunch. She was sitting in her sewing room, and I sat down in front of her to help her focus. She leaned forward and took hold of my hand. I froze. She'd never touched me in such a way. She talked about some far-off memory. As she spoke, she played with my fingers, as a child would, then grasped my hand and looked deeply into my eyes. She held my hand in hers with the love and tenderness I'd longed for my whole life.

I wish Dad could see this, I thought, blinking back tears. Then I remembered Mom's dream—and the divine nudge that brought me home. I believed it wasn't only Dad who was looking down on us now.

Mom died peacefully a few years later. When I think of her, I remember her as the mother who held my hand that day in the sewing room. It was a healing experience that I will cherish forever. That's what I had waiting for me back in West Virginia.

COME BACK, DEE DEE!

Doug Coldiron

_D_ee Dee, my Jack Russell terrier, raced after her tennis ball, her legs pumping. I'm a long-haul trucker and Dee Dee rides shotgun on my road trips. We'd been playing fetch for half an hour, relaxing midday at my company's trucking center outside of Atlanta while we waited for my next load. It had everything a trucker could need—fuel bays, shops, a lounge, even a wooded area near the edge of the property. The entire complex was bordered by an electric fence, then a chain-link barrier beyond, protection from the rough neighborhood. That's why I was comfortable having my dog off leash.

It felt good to stretch our legs near the woods. Some days Dee Dee and I never got much beyond the inside of my cab. She'd been my traveling companion ever since my wife and daughter gave her to me seven years ago. She was good company, always there for me to talk to, her tail constantly wagging. All those miles on the road never seemed that long with Dee Dee beside me.

Jack Russells are smart, curious, high-energy dogs. Intense. Something caught Dee Dee's eye by the fence. Before I could react, she let out a yelp and shot into the woods. I rushed over, but a briar thicket kept me from following. She must have been spooked to run in there! She wasn't normally skittish. "Dee Dee!" I called. No answering bark. Outside the fences, I could see cars hurtling down the road. At least there was no way Dee Dee could have gotten beyond the barriers. *I'll find her, if I have to search every inch of the complex,* I thought. *She has to be close.*

I paced the perimeter of the trees calling her name. Nothing. I alerted some of the other truckers. They volunteered to help. We searched until it was pitch black.

One by one the other truckers left. "I'll pray for you," some of them said. I wasn't so sure God was listening. I'd been praying for hours and hadn't been rewarded with even a faint bark. I was exhausted. But when I collapsed onto the bed in my cab, I couldn't sleep. All I could think about was my little dog: hungry, scared, maybe hurt. Alone.

The next morning the first thing I saw was the empty spot at the foot of the bed where Dee Dee usually slept. My heart ached. I wanted to spend the day looking for her, but there was no time. I had to load the truck and be on the road by ten to get to Virginia. Saying goodbye was part of being a trucker. But I'd never had to say goodbye to Dee Dee.

I called my wife, Rena. I'd been delaying the call, hoping to have better news. "Why don't you put up posters and I'll get something on your Facebook page? You and Dee Dee have so many people who care about you," she said. I hung up, sad. Dee Dee needed people on the ground searching for her, not somewhere off in cyberspace. Besides, it's not like I'd friended a thousand people. I used Facebook to stay connected to a few friends while Dee Dee and I were on the road. She probably had more friends than I did.

I pulled up a picture of Dee Dee on the laptop in my cab and quickly made a "Lost Dog" poster, with my phone number. I went to the office to print it and plastered copies on the walls, by the fuel bays, everywhere I could think of. As I was leaving, I spied Russ, the maintenance supervisor. "I'll keep an eye out," he said.

"I appreciate it," I said. But I knew he had his own busy job to do. We all had our hands full. Who had time for a lost dog?

I drove up I-75, the interstate rolling by in a gray haze, and reached my destination, Abingdon, Virginia, just before 5 p.m. After everything was unloaded, I sat alone in my truck and stared out into the empty parking lot, wishing I were three hundred and fifty miles south of there. Usually Dee Dee would be sitting in my lap, licking my hand. I'd scratch her behind the ears and . . . I couldn't bear to think about it.

I reached over to my laptop and pulled up my Facebook page to see what Rena had written. At first I thought maybe I'd clicked on someone else's page by mistake. It was filled with postings: "We're praying for you and Dee Dee." "Hang in there." "Trust in God." For the first time since Dee Dee disappeared, I felt comforted. Someone besides me was worried about my little dog. If only I could get back to Atlanta soon! I thought of typing that in a prayer and posting it: "Lord, get me an assignment back in Atlanta . . . NOW!" But I knew it could take weeks before I was routed through there again.

I clicked over to my company's website to find my next job. There at the top of the list was a morning pick up in Bristol, Tennessee, less than a half hour away. I scanned over to the destination. Atlanta! Could the prayers really be working?

Stay safe, Dee Dee, I thought that night as I tried to fall asleep, back at home in my own bed. She must be so hungry. Was she able to find water? Shelter? I thought of how her whole body shivered when she was cold. If only there were some way for me to know she was okay!

My ringing cell phone the next morning woke me. It was Russ. "I saw your dog on my way to work about two blocks from here." I couldn't believe my ears. Dee Dee was alive! Then I replayed his words. Two blocks from the trucking center . . . She was outside the fences! I thought about all that traffic, the run-down buildings. The guard dogs trained to attack. A little dog like Dee Dee wouldn't survive five minutes out there.

I picked up the load and headed south. I hadn't gone ten miles when my cell phone rang again. A text from a friend wanting an update. A few minutes later, another text. A trucker letting me know he was still praying for me. The phone hardly ever stopped ringing. I couldn't look at them all. I had to focus on the road and getting to Atlanta.

Around 2 p.m. I pulled into the trucking center. Russ came out. "Let me get my car and I'll show you where I saw her," he said. When we reached the spot, there were all the things I'd feared—heavy traffic, abandoned buildings—but no trace of Dee Dee. We called for her. Drove down block after block. Nothing. After an hour, Russ had to get back.

At the trucking center I borrowed a company loaner car from Cindy, the drivers' service rep, and headed out again. But as the afternoon wore on, I could feel my hopes fading with the light. Was there any place I hadn't looked?

I saw a gleaming white Baptist church with a cross out front, across the street from a row of brick houses. I'd driven by the church several times, but never stopped. There were woods behind it. I pulled up in front and walked to the trees. "Dee Dee!" I called. It was eerily quiet. I stood there for a minute, listening. Silence. Dejected, I trudged back to the car. All those prayers. Not one of them answered. Looking up to the sky, I said, "Lord, please just show her to me."

In the car I glanced over my shoulder for traffic. And there on the doorstep of one of the houses sat Dee Dee! I sped the car across the street and into the driveway then got out slowly, not wanting to startle her. I tried to calm myself. *Don't spook her* . . . "Dee Dee," I said softly, "let's go home."

She stared, as if trying to recognize me. I crept closer. All of a sudden her tail started wagging like crazy. She bolted over to me and licked my hand. I picked her up and squeezed her tight. *Thank you, God.* Other than a coating of Georgia clay, she was the same healthy, energetic Dee Dee.

We got in the car, and I called Rena. I was so happy I could barely talk. After we hung up I scrolled through all of the text and voicemail messages. There were dozens! An entire convoy of prayer warriors.

Then there was Russ and Cindy back at the center. So many people, all lifting Dee Dee and me up to God. It would take hours to thank them all. But I didn't mind.

Who knows what goes on in the mind of a dog? I'll never know why Dee Dee ran off or how she got outside the fences or what her adventure was. One thing I do know is this: We are never alone. Prayer is with us always, and God always answers prayer.

THE PIANO LESSON

Roberta Messner

I turned the key in the door of my little log cabin and headed straight for the couch. It had been another brutal day at the hospital. Nursing was hard work—everyone knew that. But I was also suffering terrible headaches. I have neurofibromatosis, a chronic condition that causes benign but painful tumors to grow inside my head and neck even after many surgeries. On bad days—days like today—my condition caused unrelenting pain, nausea, and dizziness so severe that just taking a step forward was a challenge. Worst of all was the anxiety it created. I'd burned up all my sick leave. Now I faced another surgery on a tumor surrounding my left eye socket that was the size of a grapefruit. "I'm afraid this won't be easy," the human resources manager at the hospital where I work had told me, a stack of forms between us. "With all the leave you've taken, you can't be off for more than five weeks. If you are, your position will be terminated."

Five weeks. The doctors told me post-op recovery for a surgery like mine was six to eight weeks, minimum. I was fifty and had been working at the same hospital for twenty-five years. Since my divorce a couple years back, I'd been on my own. I *needed* this job and the health insurance that went with it. What would I do if I lost my coverage?

Lord, I asked, lying there on my couch in the dark, *how am I going to handle all this?*

Give your piano away. The answer was clear and unambiguous.

Maybe you think I'm strange, but I've been talking to God all my life, like a conversation. To me it's completely natural. I knew a clear answer when I heard one, and, anyhow, I'd already heard this answer. Every time I turned to God lately—whether in prayer or while reading Scripture—He only seemed to have this one piece of advice for me.

I opened my eyes and took in the hulking shape of the big Steinway grand that sat directly across from the couch, a purchase made during better days. The piano took up most of the space in my living room, just as it had taken up a huge part of my life. It had rescued me from despair on occasions past counting. Singing is just another way of praying, as I see it, and there was no better way for me to forget my troubles and remember how blessed I was than to sit at that piano and sing my heart out. So now I was supposed to give it away? It just didn't make sense. *Seriously, Lord, I need your help here.*

The next day the pain in my head had subsided enough for me to struggle into work. When I got home that night I was exhausted, but able to sit at my piano instead of collapsing on the couch. My hands moved to the keys and started playing a soft arpeggio in B-flat: the intro to "God Will Take Care of You." By the second verse, I was singing with all my heart: "Through days of toil when heart doth fail, God will take care of you! When dangers fierce your path assail, God will take care of you!" No one believed those words more than I did. *Lord, why do you want me to give my piano away?*

I know how much your piano means to you, the inner voice I know so well said. *But it can mean more. Give it to a church. I'll show you which one.* God didn't give me any more peace in the following days. It seemed like every time I turned to him, all he wanted to talk about was that piano.

Finally, one evening while I was trying to get to sleep in spite of the relentless pounding in my head, the name of a church came to me:

Union Missionary Baptist. It was nearby. I hadn't visited it very many times, but I knew and liked the pastor. *All right, Lord. I get the picture. If it turns out they need a piano, I'll offer them mine.*

Then, the next day, I ran into a friend who I knew went to that church from time to time. "They have a pretty nice piano there, don't they?" I said, trying to make the remark sound casual.

"Yes, I believe so," the woman said. "They have a grand piano in their sanctuary."

See, Lord? The last thing that church needs is another piano. Since my divorce, it's the only thing of any value I have left. I'd be a fool to just give it away!

A few days later, I ran into another friend. We got to talking, but mercifully, my Steinway—and my dilemma—wasn't on my mind at the time. At least until she brought it up. "You're so lucky to have that nice piano, Roberta," she said. "The other day I ran into one of the women who plays piano at Union Missionary Baptist. She told me the keys have a flat, dead sound so that it feels like she's pounding on them. It grates on her nerves. Wouldn't you hate to have to play a piano like that?"

For a moment I didn't say anything. "Roberta?" my friend said. "Are you okay?"

"Yes," I finally said. "I need to tell you something." So I explained my situation about the piano and the absurd urge I felt to give it to Union Missionary Baptist. Would my friend think I was nuts?

"That's a wonderful idea," she said. "But are you sure? You're going through a lot lately. And that piano is a godsend."

A godsend. My piano was precious indeed. But it wasn't really mine, was it? It was God's, just as everything in my life—and my life itself—was. I didn't always "get" God's plan, but I knew I always had to trust it, whether it was my piano or my job or my ongoing health crisis.

"Are you really giving this piano away to a church?" one of the movers asked as they were rolling it out of my living room. "She's a beaut! All I can say is, you must be on some powerful medication." I laughed. Yes, I was ready to trust God with everything. Even my piano.

I had my surgery not long after. I came out of the anesthesia feeling remarkably strong, which was unusual. Maybe I'd be able to make it back to work under the five-week mark after all.

The next morning my surgeon came charging into my room. "Roberta, I have some wonderful news. During your surgery we got the idea to try something called platelet gel to curtail the bleeding. It's a compound that's been used with great success on the battlefield. Well, it halted your bleeding so well we were able to remove much more of the tumor than we originally thought we could without causing nerve damage. Roberta, I think this is going to be the last surgery we'll ever have to perform on you."

I'd undergone more than twenty surgeries. They'd become a painful fact of life, and doctors had said I'd always have to have them. This was nothing short of a miracle!

I was back at work well under the five weeks, feeling fitter than I had in years—especially when I sat down to play my new piano. Yep. This time I got an upright from a local dealer. He'd heard about me donating my Steinway to the church, and he gave me such a deal it was like a gift. I have to admit, it fits a lot better in my small cabin.

I won't say my health was my reward for giving away my piano. But I do know that when I trust God's loving guidance, the rewards are unimaginable.

HOMETOWN HERO

Carla Rye Faherty

*W*hen I opened my closet, my eyes immediately fell on my late brother Gary's Army uniform. The brass buttons shone, the ceremonial ribbons and pins were bright, the nameplate proudly announced RYE.

Gary Rye had been smart, kind and funny. The best younger brother anyone could ask for. In 1966, he enlisted in the Army and was shipped off to Vietnam.

I was so grateful when he returned in one piece. But the war's effects were long-lasting. He died from lung disease a few years later, probably the result of Agent Orange, a defoliant chemical used in Vietnam and known to cause respiratory disease.

As executor of his estate, I'd had the job of cleaning out his house and going through his belongings. I donated what I could to charity, but I couldn't bring myself to part with his Army uniform. Instead, I brought it home, zipped it in a plastic garment bag, and put it in my closet, where it had remained for the past twenty-six years.

Lord, what should I do with this? I wondered. I worried about what would happen to it once I was gone. I wanted Gary to be remembered. But now wasn't the time for such thoughts. I had a trip to pack for.

Recently, I'd had an overwhelming desire to travel to my hometown of Spur, Texas. I hadn't been back since my father's funeral in 1986. All of my family and friends had moved away years ago. I wouldn't know anyone. But no matter how I tried to dismiss the notion, I couldn't stop thinking about Spur. I needed to see it again. I asked my husband, Rick, if he'd be up for a road trip. He agreed. So I booked us a room at a bed-and-breakfast for the weekend.

Returning to Spur was surreal. The streets were familiar but slightly different. After we got settled at our B&B, Rick and I took a walk downtown. I enjoyed giving my husband a tour, pointing out what I remembered from my childhood and what had changed.

On our second day, we visited the museum across the street. It showcased artifacts from Spur's long history. There were photos, displays, desks from old schoolhouses. But the exhibit at the back really got my attention. There, against a backdrop of American flags, were mannequins dressed in United States military uniforms. According to the plaques, they'd belonged to Spur residents who had served their country. Just like Gary.

My heart raced. I found the museum attendant and told her about my brother, a Spur boy, born and raised. I told her that he had served in Vietnam and had since passed. That I still had his uniform.

"Do you accept donations?" I asked.

"Yes!" she said. "Most of the donated uniforms we've received are from World War II. We'd be proud to display it."

I was elated.

As we were packing the car to leave the next morning, a man on the sidewalk outside approached us. I waved. Everyone in Spur was friendly.

"Hi there," he said. "You folks visiting?"

"Yes," I said. "I grew up here. My maiden name is Rye."

"Gary's sister?" he said.

"Yes! You knew him?"

"Sure did," he said.

He introduced himself as John. He explained that decades ago, he'd met Gary in Fort Worth. Gary had applied for a role at John's company, and John had hired him. John had lived in Fort Worth for years. Recently he'd returned to Spur to retire.

What are the odds? I thought. We stood there talking for a while, swapping stories about Gary. It meant so much to me, to know that even after all these years, someone in Spur still remembered my brother. And now others would too.

My latest trip to Spur was to see Gary's uniform on display. I now understand why I was being urged to return to a place I thought I'd never see again. But I know I'll be back. Because now, part of my heart is there.

Ninety Minutes

Erica Buchanan

It was after nine on a Monday night. Outside it was winter dark. The emergency room, where I sat, was the harsh, cold white of fluorescent lights. I was petrified, my eyes bleary with exhaustion. A doctor appeared and ushered me and some friends and family members into a consultation room. The doctor's tone was grave.

"Your husband is in cardiac arrest," she said. "He doesn't have a regular heartbeat. We're doing everything we can, but his brain has been starved of oxygen for too long. He's young, so we're not going to give up. But I can't promise anything."

I could barely take in the doctor's words. For a split second my entire marriage to Jeff flashed before me. Jeff, who had brought such compassion and steadiness to my life. Who had shown me what it meant to be a wife, a mother, a woman of God. We'd weathered countless troubles and grown together in love and faith. Our eighth anniversary was just a month away.

Suddenly I remembered. Today was Valentine's Day. Was I going to lose the man I loved today of all days?

I knew I shouldn't let the news defeat me. I should pray, but I couldn't form the words. Maybe it was that I was too stunned. Or maybe it was something deeper. Who was I to think God would do me a special favor?

We returned to the waiting room, which had filled with even more family members and friends from church. I couldn't fall apart in front of them. I had to face facts.

Suddenly my thoughts were interrupted. "No!" my best friend, Allyson, declared. She waved her arms in front of her like an umpire calling safe. "We are not going to accept this. Lord, we hear the doctor's words and we honor her expertise. But we know you are the final authority. You can perform a miracle for Jeff if it is your will. We pray boldly for a miracle."

Allyson and I had met when we were both on staff at the church Jeff and I attend. Allyson headed the children's and youth ministries, and I worked in human resources. Just recently I'd given notice. Jeff and I were going to expand our promotional-product business— putting companies' logos on T-shirts and other items.

I'd always admired Allyson's forthright faith. I wanted to be bold in my beliefs like that, to put my concerns out there for God as if I totally expected him to show up and answer. My own relationship with God was more careful and conventional, almost guarded.

A chorus of Amens followed Allyson's prayer, then the sound of people adding their own pleas.

Several minutes passed. The doctor returned. "We've restored his heartbeat," she announced. "You can come see your husband. Briefly." It took all my strength to walk through the large waiting room. My mom held tightly to my left arm, and Dad supported me on my right.

I followed the doctor to Jeff's bedside. I could barely see him through a tangle of wires, tubes, and devices. I heard beeps and a kind of mechanical gasping. A machine was breathing for him. He was pale. I grasped his cold hand.

"Don't you leave me. Do you hear me? Don't you leave me," I said, trying not to cry. "You be strong."

That was all. I returned to the waiting room, my mind fixed on a single word: *Babe* . . .

That was the last thing Jeff had said to me, calling out from our bedroom. Our three girls had just gone to bed. I was sitting down to watch TV. Everything after that was a terrifying blur. Finding Jeff collapsed in the bedroom. Frantically punching 911 on my phone. Sending Emily, our middle daughter, racing to the neighbors. Sirens, paramedics, the ambulance.

I'm too young to be a widow, I thought as I found my seat in the waiting room. I was thirty-four. Jeff was thirty-nine. He'd been diagnosed with hypertrophic cardiomyopathy a long time ago. He'd always taken medication. But he'd resisted his cardiologist's advice to have a defibrillator implanted. "I'm fine," he'd insisted. I think surgery was just too much of an acknowledgment that something was wrong. Jeff didn't like being the center of attention, either.

After a long time, the doctor reappeared. The room got so quiet I could hear her scrubs swish as she walked. "I have good news and bad news," she said. "Jeff's heart is beating on its own. We're moving him to Critical Care to cool his body. Our immediate concern is whether he lives until morning. But even if he does, the loss of oxygen to his brain likely means brain damage. The cooling helps to reduce the damage. But . . . I can't predict what condition Jeff will be in if he wakes up."

I noticed the doctor said *if*, not when. Yet Allyson immediately leaped up. "Lord, we praise you for this victory!" she exclaimed. "Amen!" everyone echoed.

I kept my eyes on the doctor. It had been an hour and a half since Jeff had gone into cardiac arrest. His heart had not beat on its own that entire time. I knew that the brain can't survive more than a few minutes without oxygen. I was grateful for Allyson's prayers, grateful for her faith. But I couldn't let myself get swept up in it. I had to be realistic. I had to be cautious.

A short time later a nurse told us we could go up to Critical Care to see Jeff. Two dozen people trooped into the elevators with me. Jeff coded twice more before a doctor came to tell us they'd stabilized him and begun the cooling process.

We walked into Jeff's room and I sat at his bedside. He looked no better than before. He was still pale, still surrounded by machines. Numbly I took out my phone and texted an update to some friends, explaining Jeff's dire condition and asking for prayers. To save time I copied and pasted the same text message to other friends. Too late I realized I'd accidentally posted the text as my Facebook status. Right away my phone's screen lit up with replies as my eight hundred Facebook friends began learning about Jeff's ordeal.

Hours ticked by. To give myself something to do, I began posting updates to Facebook. Jeff's potassium level is critically low. *Pray for it to rise,* I typed.

Not long after that, a doctor came into the room. "We're not sure why, but Jeff's potassium level shot up," he said. "He's doing much better than we had expected."

I caught my breath.

"What are your top three concerns at this point?" I asked.

The doctor told me, and I immediately posted to Facebook: *Your prayers are working! Jeff's potassium is up. Please pray for his kidneys to function, his glucose to be normal and his heart to beat rhythmically.*

Two hours later a doctor announced that Jeff's glucose level was normal. "We praise you, Lord!" Allyson exclaimed. I almost said those words right along with her.

Every time I saw a nurse or a doctor that day, I asked what the medical team's top three concerns were and posted them. Every time, our prayers were answered.

Tuesday turned into Wednesday. We were gearing up for the rewarming process. At one point, I glanced out the waiting-room window and saw thirty people gathered in a circle on the sidewalk below. Friends from church, praying. Prayers were also rising from the waiting room, now packed with fifty more friends and family members.

Suddenly, over the intercom, we heard, "Code blue, room 220!" That was Jeff's room!

I ran. A dozen doctors and nurses were gathered around Jeff's bed. They managed to revive him again, and resumed the process of bringing him back to a normal temperature.

At last, a nurse told me I could speak to Jeff. It was the first time I'd spoken to him since Monday. I moved to his bedside and, leaning over his body, I put my face close to his. I took his hand. It was even colder now, due to the cooling process.

"Jeff, I'm here," I said, trying to give my voice the same authority I heard in Allyson's.

Immediately his head turned and seemed to lift up a little. His eyelids twitched as if they were struggling to open.

"Don't leave me, don't give up!" I said. "Fight, Jeff! Everyone's praying. You're a miracle."

His eyes didn't open. He made no sound. But at that moment I knew he was in there. I knew he was alive. I knew that, against all odds, he was going to be okay.

How could I think otherwise, when so many people had prayed? When so many supposedly impossible prayers had already been answered? And when God, at this moment of fear and darkness, had somehow fought through to the center of my faith and met me? At last I understood why people like Allyson pray so boldly. It's not because they feel God has singled them out for miracles. It's because they know that whenever we pray, God always shows up.

Certainly he was there in that waiting room packed with our family and friends. He was there in the prayers flying around the internet. And he was there in Allyson's voice calling us out in faith. Regardless of what happened to Jeff, I knew God held us. He held us all—Jeff and me and the countless other people whose story had become part of ours.

It has been two years now since Jeff left the hospital. He has an implanted defibrillator and is not quite as active as he used to be. But in every other way he is fully, miraculously recovered—no damage whatsoever to his brain or other organs.

We celebrated last Valentine's Day by having dinner at the heart hospital with the EMTs and hospital staff who helped to save Jeff's life. We could have invited so many more people. A far-flung community had gathered together to ask God to work a miracle—which he did, in my husband's heart and in my own.

A LOVE THAT FORGIVES

Carolyn Maull McKinstry

I sat nervously in the waiting room of a psychologist. My husband, Jerome's, plea for me to see a doctor had finally sunk in, and I had come. But not even Jerome knew the depth of my misery, how the sadness never went away, no matter how I tried to numb it with alcohol. These feelings had been a part of me since I was fourteen, throughout high school and college, going on ten years now. I kept to myself. Rarely did I talk to other people. I was afraid something terrible would happen if I got too close to anyone, even Jerome, our daughters, and other family members. I didn't know where these feelings came from. That's what made them so frightening.

I picked up a magazine and flipped through it. The pictures that stared back at me were white smiling faces. Their lives were nothing like mine. I had grown up in Birmingham, Alabama, during the height of the civil rights struggles. Our city had been nicknamed Bombingham, because of all the bombs that had destroyed black homes, churches, and businesses.

My parents had done their best to shelter my brothers, sister, and me. They may have talked with their friends about segregation and racism, but not with us. Daddy told us places we weren't to go, like across the railroad tracks, and insisted my brothers escort me everywhere. I questioned why there were so many rules. But I didn't know to be afraid, not then.

Church was the one place I was allowed to be on my own. We went to the Sixteenth Street Baptist Church downtown. I'd met Cynthia, my best friend, there. I remember being baptized at thirteen. When the pastor lifted me from the water, I blinked and looked up into Jesus's tender face in the stained-glass window above the baptismal font. It seemed as if he were telling me, "I'm here, watching over you." Today, I wondered if that was true. No matter how I prayed, God hadn't eased my suffering. Lately I slept only a few hours at night. By morning I was exhausted. I picked at food. I lost a lot of weight. My hands were always breaking out in rashes. How could I go on?

Jerome was constantly asking me, "What's wrong?" But I couldn't put the darkness inside of me into words. We'd been married six years now, with two beautiful girls. Why was my head filled with thoughts of death?

Jerome's job had recently transferred us to Atlanta, Georgia. The only person I'd met was our next-door neighbor. I found myself drinking more and more. A week earlier I'd mixed a mid-morning drink and sat down in front of the TV, just trying to get through another day. The girls were outside playing. A commercial came on: "Are you confused about life? Need someone to talk to?" It seemed to speak directly to me. "Call this number. Counselors are waiting to take your call." I dialed the number. A woman answered. She was explaining the services they offered when Jerome came in. He'd forgotten some papers he needed for work. "Who are you talking to?" he asked. "It's really early to be drinking."

I told him I was talking with someone from a suicide hotline. "I just wanted someone to talk to," I said. "I was lonely."

"I think you need to see a doctor," he said. I agreed.

My doctor referred me to a friend of his. I didn't know initially the friend was a psychologist. That's how I ended up in a psychologist's waiting room. A door opened next to me. "Mrs. McKinstry," the psychologist said. I wondered what he would ask me. Nobody I knew had ever been to a psychologist.

He led me back to a small office. He was a kindly older man. I told him I wasn't sleeping, that nothing made me happy. He listened intently, nodding and taking notes. He asked what I did during the day and if I was drinking. His eyes locked on mine. "What you're dealing with is depression. It's treatable, but you won't survive if you keep on like this. You need to face your feelings.

"I can't help but think there's something, maybe in your past, you need to let go of," he continued gently. "We need to figure out what's bothering you."

Driving home I heard his words repeat in my mind. What had happened to me? I remembered how happy and carefree I'd been as a child. Where had that girl gone?

Daddy hadn't been able to shield me from the violence that had happened in Birmingham when I was fourteen. Nearly every day I thought about my friends, the girls who'd been killed when our church was bombed. I tried not to dwell on the past, but it was always there.

I picked up my girls from the neighbor and got them settled playing in our yard. I went into the house, then to a closet where I had a box full of keepsakes. There on the top was an old black Bible. My parents had given it to me the day I was baptized. I had always carried it to church. I had brought it with me that awful day, September 15, 1963 . . .

It was Youth Sunday. I was laughing with Cynthia, Denise, Addie and Carole while they primped in front of the restroom mirror. I needed to leave. I was the Sunday School secretary. I had to get my attendance and offering report in by 10:30 a.m. I ran up the stairs. The phone in the church office rang. I held the heavy black receiver up to my ear. A man's voice said, "Three minutes," then he hung up. What was that about? I remembered I still needed to collect the report from the adult classes. I walked into the sanctuary, toward the stained-glass picture of Jesus.

Boom! The floor swayed. But the sound was muffled. Thunder? Glass fell at my feet. Someone shouted, "Hit the floor!" I dropped, flat on the ground. Silence. Then a stampede of feet. Police sirens. I had to get outside. I looked up. There was a hole in the stained-glass window where Jesus's face had been.

The streets were filled with people screaming and crying. Finally I saw Daddy behind a police barricade. We drove home in silence, too scared to say a word. How could anyone bomb a church? I only hoped no one had been hurt.

Late that afternoon, our phone rang. Mom answered it. She was quiet and solemn as she listened to the caller. Then she hung up and turned toward us, her face filled with sorrow. "There were four girls in the restroom who never made it out," she said. My friends. It felt like my heart had stopped.

"It can't be true," I whispered.

Mom nodded. "I'm afraid it is," she said. "They died."

I remembered the strange phone call at the church. Had someone been trying to warn us? Or taunt us? Over the course of the evening—through friends and neighbors, the radio, and the evening news—we pieced together what had happened. But each bit of information only left me more stunned and frightened. There were people out there who wanted to kill us. They'd taken my friends from me. Bombed my church. That night in bed I burrowed deep under the covers, but it was hours before I got to sleep. It seemed there was no place safe anymore. An awful emptiness opened up inside of me.

The next morning Daddy made breakfast, like every morning. No one asked, "Carolyn, are you okay? Do you miss your friends? Do you want to talk about what happened?" Back then, there was no grief counseling. Loss was a part of life, and you were supposed to stoically push through it. I went to school on Monday and laid my head on my desk wishing I could block out the sadness, anger, and confusion.

Now I knelt on the floor next to my closet. My body shook with emotions that had simmered inside of me for years. How could someone have bombed God's house? Killed four innocent little girls?

What kind of person was capable of such evil? They had caused so many people so much pain. I'd never even gotten to say goodbye to my friends. My parents had asked if I wanted to go to the funeral. I said no, twice. I wanted to remember them as I had last seen them. But I did want the killers to hurt. I wanted them to feel the same pain that I felt inside.

God, I prayed, I am in so much pain. Please fix my body. Take away my cravings for alcohol. Please touch me with your healing so I can go forward.

I picked up my Bible, felt the weight of it in my hands. It fell open. There was an old church bulletin tucked inside. I looked at the date: September 15, 1963, the day of the bombing. I read through the hymn selections for that fateful morning, read the page numbers and spoke the names of the people who were to give the prayers. Halfway down the page I saw the pastor's sermon title: "A Love That Forgives." There was a scripture reference, Luke 23:34. I flipped to the passage and slowly read the words: *Father, forgive them, for they know not what they do.*

Tears streamed down my cheeks. I thought of that stained-glass window, of Jesus reaching out to me. All these years I'd carried this burden, without ever once . . . *Forgive me for not coming to you before now, for not trusting you.* I tried to see the bombers as God saw them. I wept, thinking of someone so fearful that killing seemed the only option. *Forgive them as you have forgiven me.* I could feel the hardness in my heart melting, anger and bitterness flowing out of me. Then the tiniest sensation—one I barely recognized. I ran to my girls, held them tight. I wanted to remember what it was like to be young again, carefree, life full of possibility.

My depression didn't lift overnight. I'd taken only the first step of a long journey. I still had a lot to learn about the healing power of forgiveness. I kept returning to God in prayer and met again with the psychologist. From that point on I stayed as busy as possible. Every day the girls and I went bike riding. I bought cookbooks and taught myself to bake. We joined a church and I raised money for a new nursery. Slowly I began to see the world with new eyes. I reached out to others, even strangers, listening to them. I'd believed we're all God's children, and it became real to me—how loving and warm people are, how much we have in common, how it's mainly ignorance that separates us. Later, I enrolled in divinity school so I could bring God's message of love, forgiveness, and reconciliation to the hearts of all, allowing God to use me—my experiences and voice—to deliver his words.

We moved back to Birmingham in 1978 and again became members of the Sixteenth Street Baptist Church. Every day, visitors come from around the world to remember and reflect on the pivotal moments that changed a nation. They come to see the place, to physically touch it and spiritually connect with it. The church holds a special status in the history of the civil rights movement. It remains a symbol of faith and hope for all who enter its doors. For me it will always be a reminder of God's infinite grace and love for all his children, and how we are given that love in order to forgive what seems unforgivable and release our burdens to him.

AUTHOR BIOGRAPHIES

Julie Arduini is a contributing writer to several books. She lives with her husband and two children in Ohio.

Sandi Banks is Mom to six children, Grandma to ten, and gave birth to her first book, *Anchors of Hope,* in 2002.

Lisa Bogart lives in San Rafael, California, where she gains inspiration through hiking. Her favorite writing form is the devotional, and her work appears often in *The Upper Room.*

Renae Brumbaugh, a freelance columnist and author, lives in Texas with her husband, Mark, and their two children. Her book, *Morning Coffee with James,* was released in fall 2009.

Timothy Burns has written professionally for six years with deep connection to cultural, Christ-centered living. His writing spans Christian living, apologetics, and the hidden benefits of personal trials.

Dianne E. Butts writes for magazines and compilation books. She also enjoys riding her motorcycle with her husband, Hal, and gardening with her cat, P.C. They live in Colorado. See www .DianeEButts.com.

Gary L. Crawford is retired from ministry. He resides in Omaha, Nebraska, with Kat, his wife of forty-nine years, and his Border Collie, Paddy. He has written numerous devotionals. His cancer story is published in *Soul Matters for Men* and at www.PMPAwareness.org.

Blue-belt **Dianne Daniels** hopes to encourage mothers through her writing and speaking ministries. She also serves as a Christian parenting coach. Learn more at www.motheringlikethefather.com or diannedaniels.blogspot.com.

Sally Edwards Danley enjoys ministering to others as a leader with the Heart of America Christian Writers Network and with Celebrate Recovery at her church. She lives with her husband, Dan, in Kansas City.

Lisa Plowman Dolensky celebrates being married twenty-one years and loves being a mom to three miracles. She's a parochial prekindergarten teacher, writer, and University of Alabama graduate.

David Evans lives in Richmond, Virginia, with his wife and two children. God has led him in safety throughout his life, from combat in Operation Iraqi Freedom to finding his beloved wife and family.

Karen Evans lives in Palm Harbor, Florida. Karen has written magazine articles for Focus on the Family.

Mandy Foster taught elementary education for thirteen years, is a stay-at-home mom, and resides in her hometown of Tuscaloosa, Alabama. Husband Tim owns and manages two Pottery Grill restaurants in the area (Cottondale and Northport).

C. M. Freeman lives in the Northeast, is a freelance writer, and works in publishing. She is an animal lover and enjoys the beach.

Lynne Gentry is an author of numerous dramatic works, articles, and novels. She travels the country speaking at women's conferences. She counts raising two godly children as her greatest accomplishment.

Muriel Gladney has an associates degree in liberal arts, as well as a certificate in journalism.

Sandra Glahn teaches at Dallas Seminary, edits *Kindred Spirit* magazine, and has written fourteen books, including the Coffee Cup Bible Series. She's pursuing a PhD at the University of Texas–Dallas.

Linda Holloway is a freelance writer, artist, and teacher. She enjoys speaking to women's groups and can be reached at lfholloway@att.net. She and Jerry, her husband, live in Prairie Village, Kansas.

Jon Hopkins has worked with teens for over thirty-four years. He is currently youth pastor at Victory Baptist Church, Tonganoxie, Kansas, and teaches middle school at Open Door Christian School in Kansas City. He has two children, has been married twenty-eight years, plays the mandolin, and chases tornadoes for fun.

Sally Jadlow is author of *The Late Sooner,* a historical novel based on her great-grandfather's diary during the Oklahoma Land Run of 1889. She also writes poetry, short stories, and devotionals.

Linda Jett lives in Newberg, Oregon, with her husband of twenty-nine years. They attend 2nd Street Community Church where they participate in the drama ministry.

Pat Stockett Johnston has written numerous articles and columns, and several books. She is an ordained minister in the Church of the Nazarene and served as a missionary in Lebanon, Jordan, and Papua New Guinea.

Sudha Khristmukti teaches English in India and writes for Christian magazines and secular newspapers. She loves playing the sitar, listening to Western music, and rescuing stray dogs. She also has a pet squirrel and pet crow.

Mimi Greenwood Knight is a freelance writer living in South Louisiana with her husband, David, four kids, three dogs, two cats, and a fish called Gilligan. She has over three hundred published articles and essays. Mimi enjoys butterflies, gardening, Bible study, and the lost art of letter writing.

Mark R. Littleton authored more than a hundred books that collectively sold over a million copies before his passing in 2020. Among many other activities, he helped writers through Heart of America Christian Writers Network (www.HACWN.org).

Lynn Ludwick is a freelance writer who lives in a funky little house she's dubbed the Peace Cottage and enjoys family, friends, reading, and quilting.

Karen Morerod is a freelance writer who enjoys seeing God work in her life in Kansas. She teaches Bible studies and uses drama to help God's truths come alive for others. She is a pastor's wife, and a mom and grandma.

Pam Morgan is a singer, speaker, and writer from Lee's Summit, Missouri. She travels nationwide, evangelizing with her singer-songwriter husband and two daughters through song and testimony. See www.WalkingMiracle.com.

Leslie J. Payne is a retired sign-language interpreter for the deaf. She and her husband, Richard, live in Annapolis, Maryland, and enjoy family, travel, and sailing.

Donald E. Phillips is a chaplain in Lawrence, Kansas. He's also a former university professor, pastor, and author.

Jim Rawdon, a native of the western Oklahoma prairie, has experience as a chef and in the men's clothing business. At forty he became a pastor and seventeen years later began writing.

Veronica Rose (pen name) is a fairly new writer of stories and has many gospel songs to her credit, which she, as well as other artists, have recorded.

Susan Kelly Skitt writes and speaks about the adventure of life with Jesus Christ. She lives in Bucks County, Pennsylvania, with her husband and two sons. Contact her at www.womensmentoringministries.com.

David Michael Smith writes from Delaware, where he is also a marketing specialist with the Delaware Department of Agriculture.

James H. Smith and his wife, Louise, live in the Baltimore area. Currently James is writing his life story. You can e-mail him at RevSmithStory@yahoo.com.

Gay Sorensen lives in Olympia, Washington, and writes a monthly column for her church newsletter. Her poems and stories have appeared in several publications. She is a member of SoundView Christian Writers.

Jill Thompson, author of *Soul Battle: It's Not Against Flesh and Blood*, is a professional storyteller, speaker, and school librarian. Jill and her husband, Wally, live in Waynesboro, Pennsylvania, and have five grown sons.

Steven Thompson writes from his home in Osage, Iowa.

Laurie Vines lives in Richmond, Virginia, with her husband and two children. She is a freelance writer and public-speaking teacher.

Elisa Yager is mom to two great kids, two cats, four goldfish, and a bunny named Ms. Elmer. She is a manager of human resources and safety for a manufacturing firm located in Pennsylvania. Elisa welcomes your feedback at Proud2blefty@yahoo.com.

ACKNOWLEDGMENTS

To John Howard and Philis Boultinghouse,
who captured the vision for *God Encounters*.
Special thanks to Jeanette Gardner Littleton,
for all her invaluable support.

A Note from the Editors

We hope you enjoyed *God Encounters*, published by Guideposts. For over seventy-five years, Guideposts, a nonprofit organization, has been driven by a vision of a world filled with hope. We aspire to be the voice of a trusted friend, a friend who makes you feel more hopeful and connected.

By making a purchase from Guideposts, you join our community in touching millions of lives, inspiring them to believe that all things are possible through faith, hope, and prayer. Your continued support allows us to provide uplifting resources to those in need. Whether through our communities, websites, apps, or publications, we inspire our audiences, bring them together, and comfort, uplift, entertain, and guide them.

To learn more, please go to guideposts.org.

We would love to hear from you:

To make a purchase or view our many publications, please go to shopguideposts.org.

To call us, please dial (800) 932-2145

Or write us at Guideposts, P.O. Box 5815, Harlan, Iowa 51593